Three Readings
for
Republicans and Democrats

CAROL BLY and
CYNTHIA LOVELAND

with an AFTERWORD

Table of Contents

How Radiation Oncology
Nearly Made Me
a Republican

A few years ago I booked a Sunday lunch for two English friends and myself in Suffolk. They wanted to try a country inn they had heard praised. Like other retired people they were gradually getting around to all the handsome old eating places within fifty miles.

It was the last day of my annual February visit to Lorna and Eunice. We were all three grateful to have got to the inn because the day was full of rain blowing at us straight from the North Sea. Eunice and I had packed Lorna into the back of my compact rental from Gatwick Airport. Then Eunice, map in hand, trilled out directions in the still lyrical voice of an old choir treble. "Left, left, left!" she called. And "All clear! All clear! Now make your right!" She kept us on our route off the A-11 and zigzagging on narrow B-roads. She commanded me as if I and the car were a column of soldiery. Well, retired people tend to go at their excursions as if they were serious campaigns. The sky grayed and lowered with rain.

This particular lunch party, Eunice and Lorna announced, they wanted to pay at least half of.

All right, I said, we will go shares.

The inn people showed us into their warm lounge. They put us three old ladies right in front of a genuine wood fire. To burn wood is nearly an affectation in the south of England. Over the last century fireplace fuel was coal. Then came the ecologically correct "solid fuel," but in all the times I'd visited England I had never sat before a wood fire. This one was not only wood but a handsome root cluster of what must have held up a huge hardwood. You felt the engineeringness of it, the core of a whole tree giving over. Waiters brought us menus to choose from and whisky for Lorna, madeira for Eunice and sherry for me.

The rain struck harder and harder against the soldered panes, but we were inside, warm and dry. The day, the weather, the inn were any old English major's dream of the Brontes, Hardy, and 1930s weekend murders of Freeman Wills Crofts or Dorothy Sayers.

I am a cheap drunk, and what's more was not only grateful to be here with old true-hearted friends but—saying nothing of this—I rejoiced in having had a few days' break from the United States. At home I felt a low-level but constant background shame for my country's politics. Here I could be lightweight, stunned with the trusty, nearly granular sherry.

I felt resonant and intelligent. Happy. I have always loved principled people, especially principled people who carry off more self-sacrifice than I would ever even daydream about. I know it's a weakness—being that kind of follower who gloms onto admirable teachers. I know that. But having any ethical teacher or mentor to admire makes me happy. It would be hard to give up.

These two older women were friends of long standing. We had been fellow churchpeople in the idealistic, very Labour-minded St Mary's, St Lawrence's, St John's Church in Thaxted (Essex). C. S. Lewis, in one of his less exasperating diatribes, said that the best sort of friendship is the kind that binds people together who are servants of a holy cause. Whenever I could rub two cents together to visit England I went. For years and years I had sung in the winter or at Easter or Whitsun with the Thaxted Church choir, sitting and kneeling among all those leftish, idealistic friends.

The vicar was given to drama. I especially liked his forthright remarks about the greed of Conservatives since the few American clergy I knew were afraid that if an ethical issue involved more than three or four people it stopped being ethics and started being *politics* and therefore something to keep clear of. Jack, the Vicar of Thaxted, didn't keep clear of anything.

One year I had visited during a by-election. Any American Democrat, especially a liberal Democrat, does a lot of self-congratulation. It makes up for the tiresome struggle of being a liberal Democrat—sending the e-mail that moveon.com asks you to send, urging your senators toward legislation that you think would help the planet or at least others than yourself—and the unremitting discomfort of having painful subjects on your mind much of the time. Self-congratulation makes up for always feeling you ought to be protesting on an I-35 overpass or giving money you can't really afford. Self-congratulation works like a poultice for the annoyance of being a Democrat at all.

When I was in England during a by-election, Jack announced from the pulpit, "In two weeks the British people go to the polls. Some of them will vote Conservative. Yes," and he paused, "Yes, they will vote Conservative, yet they think of themselves as Christians. A confusing idea, I think," he went on, as if thinking it all over aloud for the first time. "Yes—to vote for the privileged at the expense of the poor. Very strange!"

We choir singers sat at the rear of the nave, just in front of the bell tower where the ringers looped up their ropes and sallies once the actual service started. We got a great view of everything, and like all choir members everywhere, we thought we owned the place.

Now, from the back rows of chairs in front of us, rose sharp male cries of "Shame! Shame!"

I've always loved it that the British still, in our era, quite seriously call out "Shame!" If you tried that in the United States the speaker would grin at you and say, "Hey, chill! Don't go there!" or "Don't lay some retro guilt trip on me!"

But this was England and two men in the back row were calling out "Now you've gone too far, Father Jack!" The men in their beautifully cut weekend tweeds, and their wives, then rose and filed out. We altos and trebles saw all this perfectly. If you remember the second paragraph of *Lord Jim*, Conrad tells us that Jim's father was a country padre who adjured people to be good but managed not to discomfit his conservative parishioners. That is the usual thing, of course. Jack, however, was a moralist. We joyfully admired him.

Some years passed. Fr Jack, already in his seventies when I first sang in his choir, got still older and died. Lorna and Eunice, twenty years younger, got old and moved to Southwold, Suffolk. A decade or so younger than they, I was getting old, too. Once a year or so I would go to England to spend four days with Eunice and Lorna in their retirement house, in Southwold. By now we were bound not only by idealism but by a humorous build-up of remembered occasions. We all three recalled how from a distance the bells of any church slam down their changes, but from our place in the choir we had heard their actual workings—the wheeze of the ropes going over the blocks as the bell men stretched up and swooped down with them.

The Southwold Conservatives' Club at first felt sure of Lorna because of her accent and bearing. They were shocked to learn she was Labour. By then I had begun publishing essays based on the idea that everyone is born naturally a conservative. A baby looks out for its own needs, not someone else's. Then one grows, and with luck, you should get imaginative enough to imagine needs of others, at least their more desperate needs. This all felt exhilarating to me but it was hardly new. Friedrich Schiller had said much of this in 1801. He pointed out that millions of people love *beauty*—that's no problem, loving beauty if you have enough money to educate a taste for it. But to love *justice*—or rather, to hate *injustice!* That was what divided the men and women from the boys and girls. A century after Schiller, Erikson. Sullivan. Kohlberg. Loevinger. By 1980 or so this was ordinary ethical stage-development thinking. Old hat, but since writers stick up their nose at the mind sciences, I felt lonely and heroic taking any of them on.

Well, liberal people like Lorna, Eunice, and me were always prone to feeling like sentries who stave off evil that is invisible to sleepers. The self-congratulation of it is wonderful!

I always visited them in January and February, not to interfere with their summer guests or family. Eunice and I would do miles of wind-shaken walk along the blackberry bushes in the moor. We were idealistic walkers—that is, we always went faster than was comfortable. We nearly trotted down to the nearest chilled inlet from the North Sea. We would hustle back up, like people wearing packs. We liked getting exhausted. We'd earned the right, hadn't we, to get back into the house and crowd up to the fire with Lorna and the two cats, to have a speedy tea hour, a little drop off in our chairs like any old ladies. Those mini-naps took us handily up to the cocktail hour. Then, brains brightened with whisky (madeira for Eunice) we would solve the day's *Guardian* puzzle.

I have to tell you that though both Lorna and Eunice were Labour, the English class system operated in Lorna's house just as surely as it permeated the whole island, that scepter'd isle and fortress built by Nature for herself. Against infection. The English class system got in like some lighter gas too airy-structured to be walled out. It got in everywhere. Because of the English class system, Lorna presided over the Guardian puzzle. She got to hold it on her lap and wave the pencil about, while calling out the clues to us. She had the right. She had been at Reading University and she owned that Southwold house. Eunice was the servant, because she had never got even to training college. There was an edge to Lorna's remarks as she chaired our puzzle-solving committee. Either Lorna or I got the literary and historical allusions, but Eunice invariably got all clues with question marks or exclamation points after them. Lorna would announce the clue, in the enchantingly clarion tones of Englishwomen at play, and then she'd say, "It's one of those abominations with a screamer after it, of course—come on, Eunie, one for you!" Eunice *would* call the answer.

"You see!" Lorna would shout across to me, "You see! That's our Eunice! She can solve a pun or one of those bloody anagrams from a mile off! I can't touch her!"

Of course this was praise, but all three of us knew that puns and riddles and anagrams are a low wit. Such clues were the vile aspect of any crossword. Word play, Lorna's tone said, was meat and potatoes to the working class mind.

Now, on our last day together, we drank happily in the inn's warm lounge.

Eventually a waiter took us to a large, coolish dining room where other English people were eating. They spoke in low voices, but the clashing of cutlery! Silver and metal jangled and smacked into other silver and metal all around the room. A wine steward instinctively went to Lorna, not me, for our orders. Good thing. I can't tell cistern water from well water.

We made our way through soup and fish and sheep and fragrant winter vegetables handed round again and again. A trifle of empire size, some Devonshire cream on it, but mostly custard and lady-fingers clubbed with liquor.

At last the staff returned us to the lounge. Someone had brisked up the fire. They brought us a silver coffee service to pour for ourselves. A few other parties of eaters now sat around low tables here and there; outside, the rain continued even harder than before.

Now the bill. It turned out that for all the talk of going shares, neither Lorna nor Eunice had remembered their Barclay cards and they hadn't ten quid between them. I promptly said, "May I put it all onto my VISA card and we will sort it out later—nothing easier?"

"Right," Lorna said.

"But what about the tip?" Eunice said.

"Oh, that goes right into the VISA instructions," I explained. I was already writing on the bill in its leather folder.

"Well but how *much* tip do you think?" Eunice asked. She faced Lorna, not me.

I said, "Let's see. There was the amazing service. Five, actually six, people served us the best drinks, the best food, the best coffee, and gave us the best place by the fire. How about the usual—20%?"

I glanced up to see horrified faces.

"Well, 17% then" I said. I stopped writing. All right, I thought.

Some day I will be on a fixed income, too.

If they didn't hit the ceiling! They had somehow decided between them that although we had eaten and drunk sixty pounds' worth, a two-pound tip would do.

I said a lot of stuff.

Lorna struck back with something about when in Rome. Even Eunice, whose voice went to a scrim of descant whenever there was any disagreement, turned to me very bravely and said, But wouldn't I agree, in the event, that two quid would be all right?

I couldn't credit their stinginess. Lorna remarked that this was not America.

"Look here," I said at last. "You've both voted Labour all your life. And now you want to clip six waiters?" I warmed to my fight. I told them, "I can hardly believe you two want to clip people who have given us such good service when you aren't even Tories."

That brought such a jeer from Lorna that people at the nearest tables glanced over with interest. I heard a couple of mild little "Oh I say"s from behind me.

But now my shock at finding myself wrecking a fifteen- to twenty-year friendship turned to a simple fury.

At last Lorna stopped arguing. She said in a low, crafty snarl, "Perhaps you would be ashamed to put such a small tip as two quid on your VISA card at all: is that it?"

"I would be ashamed," I said. "What's more, I won't do it."

Like RAF Fighter Command, everyone has some Finest Hour. This was mine: I said to Lorna, "How will they ever get *their* kiddies to Reading or any other university if you pinch their tip?"

Now she shouted, "I don't give bloody hell whether the waiters get their kiddies to university or not!"

This last gratified some people sitting near us. An elderly man pushed back his chair from the low table with its drinks so he could comfortably cross one leg over the other. He turned his face now to Lorna, now to me, back to Lorna, back to me, not missing anything.

"Tell you what," I said eventually, "I am going out to the car to cry for a while. You two can come when you're ready."

I finished writing up the bill and tip, retrieved my VISA card, and left.

The rain fell at an unbroken solid slant. Like any American I lunged first to the wrong side of the car, then back out into the rain and around to the driver's side. The sky went darker. This was February, at fifty-two degrees of North latitude. Soon it would be totally black. I cried a good five minutes, but all the while I felt right-minded, as the Buddhists would say.

Lorna and Eunice joined me.

Our only talk was Eunice's subdued direction giving. At one turn I couldn't make out the curb, struck it, and we got a flat tire. I got out into the rain to open the boot.

A dark, rain streaked lorry stopped. Its side bore a huge white star. Two American sergeants, paratroopers by their insignia, climbed out and offered to help. I let them. "You go back inside," one of them said. "We'll be done in a sec." I said, "No, that's OK." They were so cheerful and kind as they changed the wheel that I nearly went back to crying. I urged a fiver on them though they didn't want it.

"Look," I said. "Please take it even though you know and I know you don't want it. Take it though, would you? I have had such a terrible day! And now I have to get back in that car and quarrel with two Englishwomen. It's like a bad dream!"

"Yeah?" they said and they both laughed. 'Yeah? —OK!" One of them snapped the toy jack into its niche. The other folded up the huge bill that a five-pound note then was—handsome money. Looking at Queen Elizabeth's engraved picture you'd never get the idea that woman's family behaved themselves all up and down the moral range of human beings.

I got back in the car. "My countrymen," I thought, watching the truck pull away. No matter how embarrassing my country's foreign policies at any given time, it's still my country. And even though soldiers are by definition people who will obey even the most totally gross orders if they get them, these soldiers were my countrymen.

"Good of those chaps to stop," Lorna said as we started up again.

We began to make it up. It was the end of a friendship, any fool could feel that, but we made some civil amends anyhow.

Well, I thought, any idealist has a disappointment waiting in the wings: one day you find that the mentors you admired have slid off their pedestals. They have become just practical people, chinzing on tips. I was yet to discover the other great disappointment that awaits liberals—the day you discover that you yourself have slid off your pedestal.

Until I got breast cancer I went on taking myself and other liberals as better than Republicans. I went on admiring Republicans for what I had always admired them for—the tireless raising of money for civic beauty and the tireless raising of money for medical research. If you have a thriving chamber orchestra in your city chances are the "Friends of the Orchestra" who keep it going are mostly Republican volunteers. Rich Republican males, perhaps females, too, for all I know, give millions of dollars to their own and each other's favorite public causes. Republican women do hours and hours of cordial, exasperating committee work. They maintain the playhouse, the museum, the symphony. They maintain the public aesthetic. These women made the butt of political jokes—well-shod, bravely dieted, who appear to spend whole lifetimes strengthening their backhand rally and their serve, these ethically blithe people who find every play they see "stimulating" or "delightful" without in the least discerning what the playwright is arguing—these are the people who show up for dull but necessary meetings when they *said* they would show up. They keep promises. They notify you when they have to break a pledge.

All this is a compote of terrible generalizations, of course, but it is what I felt about Republicans I had seen working.

Until I got breast cancer, I felt superior to them. Then in September and November of 1998 I went to the Fairview/University of Minnesota Hospital to get cured by lumpectomy and radiation oncology.

At that time it was a Twin Cities posture of college-educated women with breast cancer to be loudly self-piteous and exacting of service. Even executives sometimes behaved badly to their own colleagues in their own workplaces, and then announced, "Well—sorry! But I've got breast cancer, so what'd you expect?" That was considered not only all right, but good panache, a new kind of feminist bravado. To me it just looked like more of privileged people feeling entitled to behave any way they liked.

Some of that bad behavior showed on the radiation oncology floor of our hospital. Some patients would one day denounce the technical therapy team for being impersonal and the next day complain of someone else.

In truth, the hospital staff were always wonderfully kind to us. I realized I had never in my life been treated so kindly for so many days together. In all of those seven five-day weeks, no one ever spoke to me sharply.

I was trying not to be self-centered. Cancer patients do let themselves be very self-centered. Even the born-again Christians whom I often waited with in the Naked Ladies' Waiting Room—that was where we sat about in blue hospital wrap waiting to be called for treatment—even those Christians were self-centered. They were glad to testify to their good feelings about God and one told me she had "made her peace with her cancer," an expression that revolted me, but none of the Christians would respond to anything anyone *else* said. Understandably enough: fear makes the mind curl inward and take shorter bearings on any question. Of course it does. We scared people get going round and round upon ourselves, like plant roots going round and round in too small a pot. But I was determined not to act self-centered or irrational.

Still, I freaked in my own way. One day I asked the nurses to send for a building engineer to come up to our floor to talk to me after my morning's 40-second radiation. He showed up and I led him to the Men's Naked Waiting Room, my name for where males waited for treatment in the same blue robes we women used. One of the men's walls sported a spacious oil print of a 19th century ship tearing across the Atlantic, well canted, spray flying, royals, top gallants, mainsail, the skinny forward jibs, filled with wind. It was the kind of painting that retired workmen and industrial executives do who have always wanted to paint. It was grand and it was clearly a ship and a serious ocean.

"And now look here," I said, leading the engineer to the Women's Naked Waiting Room: "Look what we got—a bowl of dead flowers. A still life. You know what the French call a still life like that? They call it a *nature morte*—dead nature. That's what they call it and that's what it is."

He said he had not heard that, but like the nurses at the station, and like the young technicians who every day picked up a little radioactive scatter from us patients, and like the head physician for radiation oncology, this engineer had perfect manners. He did not say, "Cool it, why don't you?" He did not even give me an ironical look.

"I think a Phillips screwdriver would do it," I said. "Would you please take that nice ship picture out of the men's waiting room and give them the spooky flowers and then give us women their ship for *our* waiting room." We found the pictures were riveted to the walls. I told the engineer the reason was that the whole hospital could be converted overnight into a bunker.

Fear makes people start up little quarrels with the very system (in my case, the Fairview/University of Minnesota Hospital) that is saving their lives. I thought about it that night. I heard my voice saying that crazy stuff.

Fear or not, the fact is that any 30- or 40- second activity, even radiation, that you do 35 times in seven weeks is boring. As I drove each morning from St Paul to the hospital ramp and presented my ticket for a discount stamp I felt intensely alive. I listened to extraordinary audio books in the car. But once in the actual room, lying on the gurney, properly positioned for the gantry, with the staff having thumped a fat button on the wall that tells the machine that all non-patient personnel have left—when all that has happened, and the machinery has begun its click-cluck, click-cluck, click-cluck—I was bored by the tenth or eleventh time.

I tried to stay interested. I asked one of the technicians to show me the Block room. To go into the Block room you must step on a magnetized pad so that your shoes won't carry radioactive dust here and there. The walls are covered with danger warnings of one kind of another. At the right stands a huge stove that looks for all the world like a l920s kitchen range. One grill top held a pitcher of a molten gray stuff called Alloy No. 158. It was cerebium, which blocks gamma rays. The technicians would custom-design and then gouge out a hole in a block for each of us patients. The block fits into the gantry somewhat the way film frames fit into X-ray apparatus. Then the gamma rays come charging down through the gouged-out hole, invisibly, to pierce and burn out every cancer cell in their range. I was impressed. Those technicians looked such kids to me, yet they did exacting and hazardous work. That work might years later in their lives prove to have been of mortal detriment to them.

Each morning, positioned on my gurney, I was hopeful and bored. I daydreamed. In one of my last sessions I daydreamed that a thirty- or thirty-five year old woman crept up to my gurney. How had she gotten past everyone? "Listen," she whispered, fast, "Get off there. I am in my thirties. I'm from the Bronx. I am a single mom. I have three young children. I have no insurance. I can't even afford a store-front clinic visit, never mind radiation to cure my breast cancer. You're old. You've already raised your family. You don't need to get well. I *have* to get well! Get off! Get off! Let me on!"

"You're right," I said.

I removed my left arm from the ingenious support that kept my left breast in the position cross-haired for my treatment. I sat up to jump off.

Then, my feet dangling, I said. "Actually you go fuck yourself. I want to live."

I couldn't look her in the face of course. I looked down. There were her eight thin fingers already coiled around the gurney edge like plant roots. She had got all set to pull herself up.

I added, "I have a right." Maybe that would fix her. I did have a right.

I woke from the daydream. I held still because the radiation treatment was still going, click cluck, click cluck. I said to myself, "How charming you are, Carol, how enchanting! What a principled person you are! How charming to get to be sixty-eight years old and have no real fairness in you! Oh, *talk* about fairness, yes! But wanting actual fairness, no." When push comes to shove it is the privileged who give the good push and the poor who get the good shove.

I said to myself, "You really may as well be a Republican."

At last the machine stopped and the young tech sailed back into the room. She looked into my face. "Let me help you!" she exclaimed. "Take your time! Don't be anxious," she said. "Here–take it slowly–don't fall. It's O.K., Carol."

By this time my left breast was uniformly tanned, the odd, smooth tan that people who can afford Miami in February get on their faces.

That was four years ago. I have only now just figured it out.

What makes someone act like a conservative? I finally—these four years later— have figured it out.

It is the *kindness* in their lives, the day in day out easy kindness. For forty-five days—I include the time spent with the surgeons before the radiation oncology—I experienced that kindness. I was always in the presence of highly educated, kindly spoken people. I never once in those forty-five days got yelled at or scorned. Driving to and from the Hospital parking ramp, I listened to high baroque music. And recently, too, I learned something of great interest from an audio of The Teaching Company. I pay attention, because Professor Greenberg on the tape tells us to. He tells anyone with ears to hear how Bach created such complex and beautiful sound. Bach made himself and his composing students first get the Central Idea, whatever the central idea was. Then the melody line, then the bass, and only late in the composing, attend to connectives—development and so forth.

When I was having radiation therapy I did my own writing in the afternoons. I talked only to loving family members in the evenings. I kept clear of anyone who was broke or frustrated. I let myself discard without reading all the pleas from Friends for a Non-Violent World, the National Democratic Party, Women Against Military Madness, and the New England Peace and Justice research people. After all, I had breast cancer, hadn't I? I had a right not to be hassled. I had a right. I began to live the life of those who feel entitled to not even *think* about people being decimated by other people.

For those forty-five days I was like a little kid in a very good prep school. There is no emotional ease like the ease in American prep schools. The classes are small. The teachers make it clear that we and they are all learning together, all the time. The faculty are respectful. They make each of us anxious to become whoever we long to become. When they listen to our arguments in class or chapel, you know that they are putting the best value on what we say. They treat us, not as if we are callow but as if we are human beings who show promise of becoming serious. No one makes us feel guilty if we don't want to change the world.

In those forty-five days I lived in that sort of a kindly ambiance. Anyone would want to stay in such an ambiance. Of course they would. They would want to stay in such an ambiance all their lives.

—Carol Bly

My Dear Republican Mother

M y dear Republican mother, if you came back to life so we could talk, I would want this out between us, first thing: is it or is it not all right for human beings to live on nature's old pecking order, which we usually call the "class system?"

Oh—the pecking order! In everything from hawk's-eye weeds to alpha wolves to *E. coli* bacteria to Ivy League graduates. Inherited in wild creatures' genes, inherited in human beings' capital, inherited in childhood expectations. Then, in both animals and people, taught by parents to their young as if it were a virtue.

That is where we would have our quarrel.

It would not be a mealy-mouthed quarrel, either. You were impassioned about three activities that scarcely catch the eye of less privileged people.

1. Privileged people teach their young that the pecking order— or class system—is immutable and therefore as right as need be. It is right in the way that trees and water and stars are right.

2. Privileged people exhort early discipline in courtesy and careful workmanship upon their young.

3. And privileged people teach their young the various rewards of culture: love of nature first, because that comes nearly automatically to children anyhow; love of beauty in art and music second; and, finally, the love of literature and philosophy—story as scenarios, thinking about honor and ideals, amiably talking about ideas,

in bits and pieces if not in whole systems.

When you died of tuberculosis in 1942 I was only twelve, but you had taught my brothers and me as many of your expectations as you could. We took it from you that we had a right to spend hours and hours of leisure in astute card play or reading.

We took your early training in manners. When introduced to adults we were to step forward and shake hands firmly. We were not allowed to simp or giggle the way the other girls in my Brownie Scout troop did. Because you were always ill with the most dread disease of the 1920s and 1930s, you were unable to show us much beauty in nature at first hand, but you did your best: you gave us little lectures on the beauty of nature. You gave us the gift of abstract words to use in ordinary conversation— beauty, glory, nature—words my friends in Brownie Scouts heard only in Sunday school and church. You read aloud to us as much as you could without coughing up sputum or breaking the doctor's orders about overdoing.

Streptomycin came too late to save your life. The doctor dictated intervals at which we children might visit your bedside on the third-floor screened porch. We were not to hang about too close to you. We were allowed to hug, faces turned away from your germs, but kissing was chancy. Sometimes I was allowed an afternoon nap on the other twin bed in your porch. The Duluth foghorn gave out its half-funny, half-pathetic groan at intervals in the summer. You explained to me that fog is not just fog but something dramatic and beautiful. How wonderful mist is, you told me. You told me about England's "season of mist and mild fruitfulness." Like many patients with lingering illness, you had the knack of making first-rate mental pictures. You made me see the long, red-hulled ore boats on Lake Superior. You made a little scene for me once, of the captain and mates peering through their glass-castle windows at the fog. The oreboat masters and mates weren't the only ones, you said dramatically. Odysseus had the same problem. In my recollection, you were wobbly about Aeneas and Vasco da Gama but keen and fulsome on Odysseus, Sinbad, and Magellan. You had by heart, paraphrasing, the best fog scenes of Dickens *in A Tale of Two Cities and Great Expectations.*

Since you couldn't take us children to museums, you talked about art. Even then, when I was ten and eleven, I felt you were trying to give me some invisible kit that would come into my mysterious use later, the way the gifts of Norns and flounders and other half-wild mentors are never of immediate use to the pilgrim who receives them.

In the family scapegoat system, I was scapegoated to be "creative"—that is, artistic. You authorized the maids to add my crayons and construction paper to the shopping list O.K. to charge at the corner store.

After your death, I am the one of the four children who was given your Grand Tour scrapbook, with its black and white postcard photos of great paintings and sculpture from Munich to Rome. Whatever the trip abroad in 1913 meant to you, a year after your graduating from Wellesley, I remember your emphatic way of telling me about the shiny postcard-pictures. You talked about art as if love of art would disappear in a midwest dairy field or a forest unless you stood up for it. You told me to look for the amazing little dots of light in Corot. What Turner was good at was gigantic sweeps of sky and diffused light over the tiny activities of mankind—mankind with its beached dinghies and foundering ships.

And music. When you were well enough to come downstairs before dinner, you put on records of Brahms, your second favorite to Wagner. The drop-down 78s tore around unevenly like airplanes doomed in flat spins, but they spun out the unmistakable, gallant sounds of Brahms. You taught my brothers and me that it was just barely all right to love the second movements of things, because fools loved the second movements of symphonies—dolefulness and gentle wistfulness being accessible to the most inexperienced listeners. Ideally, you explained, one listens for and then loves the *development*. Well, I hated "the development" of musical themes and I disliked your explanations about the requisite sonata structure of first movements. Like my youngest brother, I preferred Tchaikowsky's Piano Concert No. 1 to all else, and only that part of its first movement later made into a song called "Tonight We Love." Long after you died, your sister Hope told me that your true love was Wagner, and that what I had supposed was your "grand tour" of Europe had been discreetly intended as a trip to Germany to see if you were "musical enough to…" —Hope always stumbled over this part. Musical enough to *what?* At bottom, I expect, she meant musical enough to leave the upper middle class with its drinks-hour rhetoric and languid expectations in order to be a serious, artistic person.

Apparently you were not musical enough to leave your social background. You returned to America, married, and raised a family until you died at 52. But how could anyone other than a genius be musical enough to leave the half-idle, half-industrious life of privileged people? How well you presided over your little alpha-wolf kingdom, with the amiable feelings of entitlement, the manners, the complacencies—telling servants in that complacent tone, "O yes, thank you so very much, Toini—do set it down right there, will you? Thank you so very much, Marie. That'll be fine!"

I felt dread at that tone you took with the maids. Yet how *should* an ill person thank someone for kindly, briskly, doing the needed errands? Certainly I wouldn't have been happy with the 1990s informalities. "Hey, thanks" doesn't do it. "I'm like, I'm glad you brought that bundle of knitting skeins over" doesn't do it. You said aloud "Thank you very much indeed" when what you meant, innerly, was thank you very much indeed.

But I wanted you to resemble the other Brownie Scout mothers of my Glen Avon troop. Why *wouldn't* you use their informal language? You seemed so obstinate. All I wished was that you would occasionally call things *goofy* and if only! if only! you and Dad would *putz around* and tell my friends' parents you had *putzed around* all weekend and had a *fun time.* I'd have been gratified if you had left off using expressions like "lame duck" and "dog's breakfast," too. There was such harshness in your metaphors. Once we were hanging around the fireplace: someone had come to dinner. My brothers and I were listening; the adults, glasses in hand, were talking. I heard you say of some family,

"Well, the boy seemed all right, but the girl was a lame duck!" I grew confused, wondering if you were describing a brother of mine and me. My Brownie Scout friends' mothers never talked about any child, boy or girl, as a "lame duck."

You read to us from Dickens, Louisa May Alcott, Jane Austen, and Shakespeare. Literature, especially reading aloud literature, gave the formality to your everyday expressions. Shakespeare added approximately 3,000 words to the English language: he didn't subtract 3000 words, as modern American culture seems to do. When he needed a new word, he apparently made up one—the very opposite to what we do now. If the Brownie and Girl Scout parents spoke informally and inchoately in the 1940s, Americans are twice as informal and inchoate now. Paradoxically, we are today much more precise about our emotions than a half-century ago, but only in the psychotherapeutic sense, not in narrative description. I expect you would be horrified at how we have reduced our conversational vocabulary to one word in five or six. For example, the word *uncomfortable* now still means sleeping on a lumpy mattress but it must also cover

1. morally offended or outraged,
2. uneasy about a possible outcome of a motion on the table,
3. suspicious of whichever strangers have joined us at this meeting,
4. aware of having just this moment betrayed our own private values or our own socio-economic group, and finally,
5. fearful lest what we just voted for in this room may be advantageous for ourselves, but disastrous for invisible, perhaps countless others. Chamberlain, stuck in the current muck of language, would have felt comfortable with peace in our time but uncomfortable about the Czechoslovakians.

Perhaps we have this word *uncomfortable* now because in the 1990s people, at least Americans, have so much to be anguished or uncomfortable about. In your lifetime, neither Democrats nor Republicans needed to feel anguished about foreign policy. In your lifetime, the CIA was still in its Boy Scout pre-version, the OSS, a legitimate intelligence agency coordinating our terrifying war efforts in Occupied Europe. You did not know, because ordinary educated citizens didn't know, that both the Nazis and subsequently the British invaded Norway not just for seaports but for the "heavy water" (H_3O) plant at Rjukan—the major material of atomic bombs. You had been dead three years before our own country—not an enemy—dropped atomic bombs on human beings. So your time was more "comfortable," and you exercised the right to use strong language. The lively Nebraska author, Mari Sandoz, reported her father's and her own irritation with the cotton-batting language of the Scandinavians when they began pouring into this pioneer country. Anyone educated to exact language trembles with irritation at the softsoaping of less forthright speakers. Of course you would never eschew calling someone a "lame duck" in favor of calling her just "goofy." Perhaps some of your scary sharpness was a reaction to the prevalent culture.

You died in 1942, at the height of American patriotism. You were either ignorant of or in impressive denial about notable sins of commission and omission of the United States between 1781 and 1942. You did not know or chose not to be conscious of the fact that the National Guard fired on striking autoworkers and coal miners. You probably barely noticed Kristallnacht and didn't focus on the fact that the United States did nothing about it and in fact closed its door to Jews trying to leave Germany. In your lifetime, lucky people, even though educated, were not expected to *double -think* the morals of the country. Genuine intellectuals were critical enough of the United States, in the 1920s and 1930s, goodness knows, but not *half-intellectuals*, drawingroom intellectuals—people of privilege with some taste for, rather than discernment in, the arts and the habit of discussing things over drinks. A more or less educated intelligent woman in 1942 might well worry about the safety of one or another of her sons, but she didn't have to feel "uncomfortable with" disastrous, oddly puerile foreign policies of her own country.

You practiced courage about your long illness. If you lived now, I think you would be brave enough to look at the bad ways the world goes round and be more than "uncomfortable" with at least some of them. You might no longer vote Republican. You would be willing to look at tough facts of the moral kind. You had the habit and the knack of courage. I think you would look at class cruelties square in the face and be willing to suffer. Besides, I need to be tolerant. If it were 1860, I bet that I would not be stirred myself to object to slavery. I bet I would have just slid along with others of my safely Northern background—the very behavior I didn't like in you.

From 1978 to 1981 I finally learned to grow up and look straight at bad news and keep looking at it. Like most children who spend more time with maids, teachers, and Scout leaders than with their parents, I knew how to make use of mentors. Psychotherapy suited me. My psychotherapist showed me how to eject a good many old family lies—a great relief—what the poet Denise Levertov called, in her poem "Modulations," "the luxury of unlearning old lies." I learned that one must name an evil if one thinks something is evil because identifying evil is vital to life, whereas denying cruelty, or shamming, in order to preserve a familiar relationship with the perpetrator of the cruelty is a psychological version of suttee.

Naming evil was unfamiliar to me, as it was for nearly all people brought up in the liberal arts. People of my background were expected to be tactful enough to follow an argument without coming the heavy; they were to be alive to beauty, and to have the sense to center themselves stoutly in their class mores.

You and I would start our conversion here. My psychotherapist was cross at me for not "coming to closure" with my anger toward you. "Nonsense," I told her. "Closure," for one thing, is some of the schmooze language that Jules and Mari Sandoz would have disdained and I disdained it, too.

"Oh, but I wish your mother hadn't died so that you and she could come to closure!" Chris exclaimed.

"I don't wish that," I told her. "My mother was a bully, and although I may be a bully as well, I will always feel the bullying in her. What good would come of our talking about her bullying? She had such a way of bullying us children if we failed some goal of hers! She would even bully us over whether or not we had had a daily bowel movement. She bullied any of the maids who spoke in the least plaintively. She bullied anyone who interfered with any of her expectations." I waxed quite rhetorical, as fools do, especially during first and even second and even third sessions with psychotherapists. (Later, of course, one settles down to being simple, telling the truth, and learning what one can.)

"Nonetheless," the therapist said, "I wish you had come to closure. I don't mean denial," she added carefully. "I mean closure."

The least I can do, then, is write this letter. I shall list some of your marvellous virtues, my dead mother.

You had physical bravery. In the Great Duluth Fire, you took your car again and again down into the smoke-laden downtown area to pick up people. They crouched on the running boards, clinging to the car as you drove up the hill and out Woodland Avenue to safety.

You never, not even once, complained to us children of your struggle with tuberculosis. When my eldest brother was two you caught TB from your father. Then you had three more babies at intervals your doctor prescribed. You raised all four of us despite coughing spells, despite constant fear of a spontaneous pneumothorax (collapse of one or both lungs), in constant fear lest we children test positive on the Mantoux tests. You spat up phlegm and blood, trying not to let it happen in orthodontists' offices or railway dining cars. You occasionally went through appalling pain. You had to endure bed rest, alone, without Dad, on the third-floor sleeping porch in summer and fall, in the third-floor bedroom winters, long stays in sanitoriums in Minnesota and North Carolina. Your doctor, in his wretched 1930s wisdom, did not allow you to breast-feed your children. A hundred times I thought of you with pity as I freely nursed mine.

A third virtue, one presently endangered in our species: motherhood. You were a thoroughgoing mother. You weren't well enough to do housework. You couldn't do the cooking—cooking, the classic arbiter of motherhood. From your bed, however, you *could* knit and mend, provided Toini or Marie or one of us children brought you the wood-handled knitting bag and your mending box. All this equipment lay on your breakfast table, once the blue Wedgwood breakfast set had been carried away on its tray. You wove elegant khaki patches onto my brothers' knickers, and taught me, too—seriously, as if I were an apprentice. How much I appreciated that! Apprenticeship is one of the dearest roles of childhood—not just watching Dad or Mother, but being taught a hands-on trade. I didn't much mind your conscious superiority about it: your mending was better than ordinary women's mending. You made that clear. I didn't mind because I was being initiated into the superior women's group. Any child can be corrupted that way. Hand sewing, making oneself do it well, not loosely, may be a thousand ways different from the Landswehr or Hitler Jugend training, but the same psychology operates: children will exert themselves hard and longer than is agreeable to them if they feel they are being groomed to do better than others.

I swore I would knit all of my children's mittens some day. I would patch their clothes. You were nearly godlike, sitting up in one of the many silk bedjackets given you, with your balls of yarn on the white counterpane. The counterpanes—a piece of household goods I have never had in any house of mine—had little alternate columns of seersucker and plain weave. They were always utterly white, because the maids washed them twice weekly in very hot water and bleach, to kill the TB germs.

First-rate menders, you told me, wove all patches precisely at right angles. The warp and weft must cross over and under one another at 90 degrees or the patch would look like a dog's breakfast. The implication, as with everything you taught me, was that one must hold the fort of superior standards against the mediocre work of the many. I couldn't argue with you. The other mothers of my Glen Avon church Girl Scout troop did patches on my friends' clothing that *did* look like dogs' breakfasts. Crafts enthusiasts often have a tinge of contumely about them. I didn't like your superior attitude, but that doesn't mean I didn't catch it myself. As Marianne Moore said, in "In Distrust of Merits," we are not good enough for our vows.

You were a first-rate conversationalist, somewhat stuck in conventional male-affirming legends. As I look back on the kinds of stories you chose to tell and read to us children, I suppose you would be a prize 1990s Joseph Campbell buff if you were alive. You took seriously the Nordic legends that Thorstein Veblen referred to as "theological underbrush." You told me about Odysseus's making the crew tie him up against the sirens' seductions. You skipped a little lightly past the virtues of Freya, because you were a tomboy and preferred the regressed Alberich and beautiful Siegfried. But like most tomboys, you admired fierce motherhood—fierce motherhood often meaning the protection of young spirits from ignoble or separatist fathers. It was the mother lion and wolf whom you admired, not the philandering male. You repeatedly reminded us children that Siegmund first learned about disinterested love from watching wild mothers and their kits or cubs in the German forests.

You were brave about your palpably approaching death. You had longed to believe in an after-life but couldn't. Your parents had been agnostics before you. I wish you had read outside the conventional canon of Wellesley graduates in literature: you might have come across Jens Peter Jakobsen's *Niels Luhne*, a book that Rainer Maria Rilke carried around with him. The last sentence of the novel is: "And then Niels Luhne died—the difficult death." I knew that you had pathetically inquired of your Wellesley friends for any spiritual hope they might offer. One of your classmates, a Buddhist, wrote out a little book of prayers for you. I have it. I am saving it to read when I am dying of something, to remind me of both her kindness and your classy bravery.

I want to list more of your virtues, but I don't know them. I was only twelve years old when you died, but had by then spent several winters away, with relations in the South. You wrote me any number of witty letters—the usual fare of sanitorium patients' letters—stories of patients who received boa constrictors in postal packages from other patients and the like. My aunt made it clear to me that you were "a terrific correspondent, with your witty narratives" but I felt chagrined: I didn't always get the point of the ironies. I was too young, or not bright enough, for your wit. I felt grateful, but underqualified.

And a low reservoir of enmity lay between us from when I was about eight years old. I blame it partly on my little-kid cowardice and partly upon your unswerving espousal of the two-class system—nature's pecking order dressed up as a logical entitlement of Hill School and Asheville School and Abbot Academy graduates to feel superior to others, without these graduates' necessarily doing a lick of work to change the world.

My cowardice: my brothers, but not I, since I was the youngest and the only girl in a gender-role-oriented family, were trained for sturdy character. It was they, not I, who obeyed our father's admonishment: do not say or do things that "would worry Mother." I constantly sneaked up to the sleeping porch on the third floor to worry you with one or another woe. You responded to me kindly enough, but at the same time I often saw your hand creep out over the counterpane, feeling for the little globe of your call bell. You rang for a maid to fetch me away again because of the doctor's orders about "complete rest and fresh air." I was disgusted with myself (as were my brothers) about my persistently worrying you, but I couldn't keep clear. If daughterhood is an addiction, I had it. Even as I flung myself up the forbidden staircase to your sleeping porch I knew I ought to stop and tell myself something along the lines of "Just shut it up, you silly clot [language from the admired E. Nesbitt]—have pity upon your mother, not upon yourself for once!" But I couldn't. My interest was for myself.

When you cried out one night, the youngest of my brothers rushed up the stairs from our bedroom floor to the sleeping porch crying, "I'm coming, Mother, I'm coming!" He was only twelve or thirteen. He had great sweetness of character. [One in our series of maids had told me that he was the best of us four children, and in her opinion it was a real shame that we others were not so unselfish as he.]

Instead of going up to you then, I hovered at the bottom of that flight of stairs. I did not want to see my mother screaming.

My heart was engorged with cowardice. I felt then that I would never live down such a cowardice. Because I was too cowardly to do what seemed to be expected, I was angry at you. What right had you to be ill, anyhow? I knew, intellectually, that you had not voted to have tuberculosis. I knew better then, but still exclaimed to myself, Why couldn't someone else's mother be sick and mine be well? "Not in my backyard," we would call such feeling now. I was a Nimby.

My being a coward, however, did not make you an angel. For one thing, you were more anal-oriented than any other human being I have seen in sixty-seven years of life. You were more anal than any of the personae of the classic 1950s jokes about anal-retentive people. None of us, not you nor Dad nor, of course, any of us children, nor the maids, knew any psychological theory. Norman O. Brown had not yet written *Love's Body*, the definitive book on *excrementum* as a spiritual reality. As late as 1970 my middle-class father still jeered at Freud without having looked at any of Freud's work. Of us four siblings, I am the only one, in fact, who has taken seriously any post-Freud philosophers of psychology.

You were stuck on whether or not each of us had a daily bowel movement. The last time you ever interrogated me on the subject, you sat on the toilet seat cover in the children's bathroom, asking me if I had had "a movement" that day. In our family, all movements, excepting those of Brahm's, Beethoven's, and Tchaikowsky's symphonies and concerti, were bowel movements. The first time I heard the expression "the movement of the clock" I grinned filthily.

"But if not this morning, surely yesterday?" you said, nearly pitifully.

"No, Mother," I said. I wielded the innermost weapon of a child against intrusive parents. Whatever else parents can do to us, they cannot without physical abuse make us move our bowels if we decide not to.

You frequently reined in the loose, Virginia-Woolfish shawl collars of your dressing gowns; surely, having such modesty, you should have acknowledged that others might value theirs.

"Darling," you said, "surely the day before yesterday? Surely you had a movement the day before yesterday?"

"No," I said.

"No *what?*"

"No, *Mother.*"

Next a surprise—and one of the most memorable moments of my childhood. You broke into tears. Your weeping was quiet but it went on.

Then, for the first time, I forgave you for intruding on my privacy. My heart went out to you, although I still balked, braced, on my short legs before you. For the first time I felt compassion that you were ill, constantly ill, always ill. Just in that moment I realized a certain truth as well: the family tradition of saying "when Mother gets better..." was only a ritual of denial. As I watched you cry I realized you were not going to get better and you would soon be dead. And for the first time I felt how your illness had its harsh claws hugely, deeply, in your body. I realized how horrible it was for you. In that moment I stopped merely resenting that you weren't a vivacious, permanented member of the PTA who, like other mothers, would chair a scary stall at the Washburn School Hallowe'en Party. I got the point of your suffering for the first time.

So I ordered my stiff legs to make the two steps forward to kiss you—not to be kissed, but, for once, to give a kiss—in kindness.

But then you said, "Now see what you've done!"

I stopped cold.

You looked right at me and said, "Now...you have made Mother cry!"

I don't blame you for passive-aggressive manipulation. One can't blame people for behaviors not yet even identified and classified by their generation.

The maids—a string of them from before I was born in 1930 and onward—came from farm towns—Aitkin, Floodwood, Moose Lake, all within two hours' driving of Duluth. Generally awfully nice girls, they would start working for us at age 14 or 11 or 16. They worked for our family two at a time, one doing most of the cooking, the other doing most of the casual housework, the two joining for the heavy housework. They both served at dinner every evening. They both spent all day Monday doing the family laundry and Tuesday ironing clothes and mangling the sheets. Their sleeping room, between our basement level and the first floor, was so damp that if one of them left a cup of coffee overnight, a gardenlike moss greened it by morning.

The maids waked us, made our breakfast, sent us off to school, and saw to it we bathed at night. Except for dinner, which was always planned by you, our meals were the maids' choices. We children had their love of soft white bread, Spanish rice, fried Spam once Spam was invented, macaroni and cheese, hot dogs. Whenever you were doing a stay in the sanatorium and Dad took his dinners with you there, the maids dropped all the rib roasts and Yorkshire pudding and roast legs of lamb off the menu: we all crowded around the kitchen table, eating meatloaf and catsup, frankfurters and hamburgers, which to this day symbolize to me affectionate nourishment with no double messages.

Of all the maids I was especially fond of Marie and Toini. One day Toini was moping at the kitchen window. Some clothes were boiling in a Hi-lex solution. The dog, Bruce, lay with his jaw leant against a stove leg. The kitchen smelled of steam and dog. Toini looked out over the gravelly driveway. She said aloud, "I feel blue." Her uncle had died. I had to guess what feeling *blue* meant, since it was new to my vocabulary. I raced up to you although we had been told not to bother you at that particular time. "Toini feels blue," I reported.

"Blue!"

"Toini wants to go home to her uncle's funeral."

You remarked, "Toini will have to pull herself together."

One maid, however, was vicious. Inez used to spank my brothers in the basement-stairs landing near the telephone. She felt safe beating them there because they wouldn't cry. But she took me down to the cellar and into the fruit room, since I shamelessly screamed. My designation in the family, remember, was just Artistic or Creative, not Strong of Character like my brothers'. Inez locked me in position across her lap. Then she swung away at me. Inches away from my face stood our family canning, the jars spaced neatly along the white shelf paper. I could see the jars' wire springs, the fading labels in my grandmother's elegant script. Gooseberry Conserve, 1934. Current Jam, 1936. Apple Jell, 1936. Years later, when I was married, my good-hearted mother-in-law offered me all her old canning jars, but they had those steel clamps. I bought my own Ball self-seal tops and rings instead.

Once Inez was at me so long I had trouble breathing. From the other end of the basement hallway, we both heard my father's car on the gravel, driving up into the garage. I escaped. I expect Inez was glad enough to see me go, too, so she could scurry upstairs to the kitchen and pretend to be helping Marie with dinner. "One of these days," Marie told her, as she reported to me years later, "you're going to get caught! You'd better watch out!" Marie did not inform on Inez to my parents, however, because young hired women's mores did not then include making interventions. Loyalty to colleagues is a basic mammalian behavior. In lions, we call it species loyalty or pride loyalty. In human beings it has several names: old-boy or old-girl network, Cabinet loyalty to the president, sticking with the team... Moral developmentalists sometimes call it Stage II behavior—a kind of live-and-let-live philosophy within the tribe. Whistle-blowers are people who have overcome such pack psychology.

I tried to explain to my dad though I had not yet recovered my breath.

"Oh, no, Dear," he said. "I know that wouldn't happen." Then he added the usual refrain, "Try not to worry Mother with it."

But one day the police caught up with Inez. Inez had stolen from The Glass Block and other Duluth stores, using various employers' charge accounts. I was delighted to hear that she was going to prison. Perhaps the police would beat her. Children are not very clear about what the police can or cannot do. I had no idea that in the 1930s, when I was a child, Southern police did indeed beat black people but not white people. I did not know that Northern police also clubbed people, but generally those people were labor union picketers. I did not know that the National Guard had been called out to fire on striking autoworkers and striking miners, but I did have a romantic idea that with any kind of luck the police would beat Inez. At the same time, I should have preferred that she be arrested for child spanking rather than just charge-account theft. But of course I didn't know that in the 1930s mild child abuse, even of Republicans' children, was not yet a crime.

Dad had a scrupulous businessman's hatred for crooks, especially for crooks who had got the best of him.

"Well, Inez should go to prison for being mean to kids," I said.

He said, "I don't suppose that she was ever mean to kids."

I reminded him about the basement landing and fruit cellar beatings.

"Oh, I don't suppose anything like that happened, Dear," he said.

One spring, when you could still travel, you and I were returning home to Duluth on the overnight train from Chicago.

I loved the train's departure. It was six fifteen in the evening. We had not even reached Evanston yet. The train ground away on its bearing surfaces. We were on a neatly made elevated track above the slums. Coal smoke from our engine shrouded and stroked people's sheets hung to dry between backyard shacks and tenement wallhooks. Children my age glanced up at us.

"Do people like living there?" I asked you. We sat opposite each other in a Pullman section. My heart was full of the usual happiness of riding trains. I knew the drill. After a while we would go to the dining car—not easy, since you sometimes coughed up phlegm during meals and other people would glance at us. We would sway left and right with the other diners as the train lurched along. We would lift our heavy forks and knives with the Chicago and Northwestern Railroad logo engraved into the silver. My white napkin was as heavy as a whole sheet. While we ate the porter would make up the Pullman car into its sections of berths, upper and lower. You and I would have two lowers, with their magical dark green beize curtains, each a little bed as secret as the bed of Scrooge.

North of Evanston, our train passed long strings of slatted carriages in which animals were being taken south to the stockyards. On a previous trip, I had asked you about those animals. "They do not know they are going to die," you said gently. There was no edge to your voice as there was when one asked about unlucky human beings.

"You must listen for the clunk clunk clunk of the wheels going over the rail-section ends," you said with a wonderful smile. "That is the characteristic sound of trains." You explained that rails were not exactly abutted because the iron must shrink and expand.

Because you taught me to love that sound, I have paid attention to it on trains from Oslo to Geilo, from Frederickstad to Berlin, from London to Audley End, Essex. Sometimes, even, even now that I am in my early old age, I notice the especially worn sections of Interstate highway 35E between St Paul and Sturgeon Lake, Minnesota: my car wheels go thunk thunk thunk over the frost-gouged concrete section ends and nostalgia is alive in me a good two or three minutes before I recall why I am feeling so touched.

You got the point of beautiful moments no matter how trivial. You said, verbatim, *Treasure up whatever lovely moment comes along*. You were never a fool. You knew better than most that death comes, welcome or unwelcome. What's more, death, you knew as well as anyone, sends its lieutenants, sickness or degeneration, out ahead to forage. Death brazenly takes stock of us when we are only minding our own business, raising our families on Dickens and *The Boy Scout Manual*, on Louisa May Alcott, on lonely agnosticism. You were a dab hand at taking happiness in such swift shafts as fell upon you.

So I was happy in the train. I looked out over the train smoke and the hundreds of shoddy backyards going by below. Most of my mind glowed with anticipation of sleeping in my Lower that night. Only absent-mindedly did I ask, "Do those people like living there?"

You said, "You know better than to ask a question like that."

Perhaps you meant that I was tactless. If the rich once start imagining how the poor feel about the slums or other depredations of the world, the rich will have traded in their complacency for moral consciousness, and who of them needs that? Dickens pointed out, any good club secretary knows enough to dispatch a servant out and round the front of the building to banish such starving bums as might press their noses against the leaded panes. "Gentlemen, God rest you merry," the carolers say, "may nothing you dismay," not "God wake you up to civic awareness, Gentlemen..." *Real politik* teaches that when the poor do have the grace to "pull themselves together," as you had wanted Toini to do, then others, the regular people, our sort, can enjoy their pleasures more fully.

I felt angry with you. In the very next moment, however, I drank the potion of immunity you offered. I actually congratulated myself on being someone entitled to travel in a train, as opposed to someone who deserved only to live in slums. Years later I read Chekhov's remark that seeing others in pain gives the rich a "flutter." I felt that extra fillip of pleasure that afternoon. At the same time, I knew it was foul. I felt the foulness of it. I delighted in the foulness itself, the way a child who has spent dozens of mornings in Sunday School delights in going with a bad boy who busts streetlights. Or the first time you enjoin your friends to bully some kid at recess. There's fun in evil. A question to pose bomb setters and militia sharpshooters: Wasn't it rather fun—the planning of it, the anticipating, then pulling it off?

I suppose I shall always feel disdainful of your bullying, small scale though it was. Yet your bullying helped me make two important decisions in my life. You turned me from drawer-of-pictures to writer-of-stories. And my memory of your complacent discounting our maids' feelings made me later vote, with the exception of my liking Eisenhower, Democratic.

At nine I wrote a novel called *The Adventures of Hilary Melwheel.* Melwheel was a hero of the American Revolution, but

when young he was beaten by his parents. My entire novel con-
sisted of two sheets of typing paper, each folded in half, torn
along the folds, then folded again into quarters. I had common-
pinned the signatures together through the spine. There is no joy
like that of having made a book, so I carried it up to your bedroom to show you.

You amiably began to read aloud. "And then they wiped
Hilary," you read aloud.

"Whipped," I corrected. "They whipped him."

"You want two p's to shorten the i," you said. "And you need
an *h* after the w to get the *whuh* sound in *whip*." Your Wellesley
B.A. had been in English.

You read on. Like Hitler, Melwheel was a battered child who
rose to amazing leadership. On page 2 you found another beating.
"Then they wiped him again," you read aloud.

Before the middle there was another wiping, or whipping.
Again you read it aloud as "wiping."

I did not say to you, "Since you know my intentions you might
have the generosity to pronounce the word as I intended it pro-
nounced." That would have counted as opposing Mother, *a subset
of the forbidden* "worrying Mother."

Later I decided that you bullied out of fear for our family status. In the last winter of your life, we visited you at Nopeming, a
TB sanitorium near Duluth. We children stood outside in a -20° F.
wind. The nurses wheeled you to a window so you could talk to
us. My brothers were brave about the cold. They told you whatever adventures they could think of from their basketball games,
their prep school and college life in general. I huddled shamelessly, and had to be told twice, sotto voce, by Dad to stand up
straight and smile at you and not keep turning my face out of the
wind. There was your face, glowing and roseate with the typical
low-level fever of tuberculosis, your head and chest swaddled
with extra blankets so you wouldn't catch cold from the open
window.

Suddenly you said, "O no, Carol! Not glasses! You don't wear
those glasses all the time, do you?"

I did, because that was 1941 and I was eleven, typically the age at which American children get nearsighted, though not then in such numbers as they do now.

I had been taught not to lie. "I am supposed to wear them all the time," I said.

"But you don't really have to wear them, do you?" you exclaimed. And then you added, looking at Dad not me, "No one in our family has ever had to wear glasses! It must be a mistake!" I recalled, with dread, your having long before called some little girl a lame duck. Wearing glasses might not be so bad as being a lame duck, but it sounded something like.

So there was a two-class system! Those whose children had to wear glasses and those whose children were just naturally entitled to 20/20 vision.

———————————— // ————————————

I did not see you again. The war took one brother into V-7 training, another eventually to Camp Devon and Fort Bragg and to Somewhere in North Africa, then Somewhere in Italy—what was called "the European Theatre of Operations." The youngest joined the fourth form at the Asheville School and I was sent to an aunt in North Carolina.

Nothing in your life led you to change your class ideals. But who ever does change class ideals unless forced? If 1998 were 1942 (the last year of your life), perhaps I would be a Republican, too. Perhaps I would deny any American history that was cruel. If 1998 were 1942, I would probably be as simple as I was at twelve, proud that Americans were going to defeat Germans. Germany needed to be beaten and American men and wealth were going to do it.

The peculiar, complex wisdom of the 1990s, family-systems thinking, was not even thought of when you were alive. How could you possibly have guessed that models, actual conversations, would be invented to help family members treat children with respect, rather than irony—ways to empower children to notice and call evil evil when they see it.

But that was then, as the social workers say, and this is now. Why should a woman of sixty-eight beat her head against her long-dead mother's politics? How absurd it sounds! Somerset Maugham said, "If one loses one's temper at every human folly one will live one's life in a constant state of ire."

Maugham was not a change agent, however. Whether or not one wants moral change lies at the bottom of most quarrels between mothers and daughters. If children do not butt their heads against their parents' class values, then those class values will keep fattening and fattening through more than the proverbial seven generations. How we all wish that German children of the 1930s had butted their heads against their parents' class values! Coming to one-on-one "closure" with a mother is chickenfeed compared to the old and the young working together for change.

If we each deliberately list our dead parents' virtues, then, without indignation, list their failures next, and then,—most important of all—list *those evils they neglected to countermand in their time*, then we can drop a good deal of the schtick about "roots." We can act like a Shadow Cabinet, watching the doing of humankind, identifying which changes to make should we get into power.

I shall always take exception to your feelings of entitlement. If I had turned out a painter, I might have forgotten all such quarrelsome stuff, but writers are writers: we lean toward philosophy.

At our best, we writers keep in mind how mysterious a mother is! Any daughter of even the skimpiest insight would recognize the fortitude of a parent like you. You took such pains to do what you could for us children. Between fits of coughing you taught me how to work hard with my hands and to love beauty and to get a kick out of small moments. You did all you could not to let any of your children make a dog's breakfast of their lives.

—Carol Bly

The Savage Stripe:
How a Privileged Teenage Daughter Changed Her Dad

"Of course we don't think of ourselves as intergenerational terrorists. We see ourselves simply as rational investors, as producers seeking profits, as consumers concerned with cutting costs, as taxpayers opposed to higher taxes, as business people and legislators eager to improve the economy and business climate of our state and nation. It is for these reasons that we opt for nuclear power, oppose stricter controls on pollution, and water-down or defeat legislation designed to curb chemical dumping and careless toxic-waste disposal, the production of greenhouse gases that cause global warming, and so on through a long but now-familiar list."

"Our distant descendants see us differently. In their eyes we are, or were, terrorists of a peculiarly savage stripe. Now let us imagine that historians in the 25th century want to know how their ostensibly civilized 20th and 21st century ancestors came to think and act in ways that are so savage and so destructive of their descendants' health, safety, and well-being. The story, as they reconstruct it after extensive research, might go something like this. Our 20th and 21st century ancestors weren't evil; they did not intend the harm that they have caused us and our children, rather, they were inattentive and short-sighted; they weren't *paying attention*—they weren't thinking about anybody but themselves and their children."

—Terence Ball, Professor of Political Science at Arizona State University, in *Duties Beyond Borders: The Expanding Ethical Universe*, The Joan and David Lincoln Center for Applied Ethics, 2002

W e will practice what we preach. If being able to imagine *other* is the first of the two steps of altruism or civic decency, then imagining someone other who may actually be some part of ourselves may be all the more useful. The second step of altruism or civic decency, of course, once one has imagined how life is for one's victims, is to decide to quit harming those victims. We will look at how to imagine victims and how to imagine oneself. As for imagining the *other* which may be partly or nearly ourselves, here is a very nice and spirited family. Let's look at them. Let's look at them with heightened interest because Dad is CEO of a company which owns several other companies, and has a fiduciary role in nearly 180 other companies. Dad is a very nice guy, too, but he and his family are having a fight this evening. The Goodnows have been having the fight in one form or another all this Saturday afternoon. This is not at all a crisis for this family: the Goodnows have had this same fight so many times since the two children passed the age of 14 that the fight itself is nearly, as Dad—that's Allison Goodnow—wryly told Barbara, his wife, part of their family solidarity.

Allison is always talking about family solidarity and God knows he has a right to: he has attended more girls' 1000- and 2000-meter races than anyone else in Norfolk County, which meant driving up to Andover on either one of the two murderous roads out of Boston. He frequently inveigled business colleagues to go with him, with the idea they'd hash over policy in the car to and from. Whether Kimberly, the daughter, placed or came in last (athletics freaked her and she wasn't much good at any of it), at best placing third, at worst being the last, she was always a girl who kept running the whole course like mad, face full of blood, eyes burning with sweat.

Dad always leapt to his feet on the little hill near the finish and howled, Way to go, KIM! His business colleagues grinned when he screamed. They knew they were being very nice guys indeed to show up for Allison's young Kimberly, but they had another feeling besides virtuousness: it was just plain a great thing to have your CEO be a loyal and passionate family man. These guys, like anyone of fifty or sixty who has worked thirty or forty years, had here and there worked for serious scum. So Allison's colleagues, when Kimberly looked like getting it together to take a white or a yellow, they, too, would shout. All *right,* Kimberly! All *right!* All *right!*

That was then. Now is two years later and Kimberly is the instigator of the regular horrible family fights. She is nineteen, a sophomore with a declared major in Psychology at Yale. It is mid-June. The air on the flagged terrace is fresh, and the Norfolk County summer air had not yet gotten thick and smelly, as if already breathed by gorillas. "Thanks, son," Allison said when his younger child, Brew, now 17, made the smart-ass metaphor about gorilla breath.

Allison offered around drinks. Barbara and Brewster got the canapés onto the low stone table. Kimberly had made the canapés, beef kidney wrapped around with bacon and broiled, "wonderful stuff, darling," her mother said, but Kimberly refused to pass them around. "That's that shit class thing of yours, Mother," she remarked when her mother had said, "Oh, take the tray with the canapés out, would you, darling?" "Ask Brew, Mother," Kimberly said. "He's the baby. It's the baby of the family who's supposed to walk around and serve whatever you're having with your nightly alcoholic fix."

Barbara pulled up, in the middle of taking off her steak-spatter apron. "Darling, I really object to 'our nightly alcoholic fix.' I do not call having two drinks, hardly ever three, before dinner on the terrace, by way of helping Dad relax after his day a 'nightly alcoholic fix.' Really, Kim, really!"

Her daughter eased herself off the edge of the kitchen work surface and put both arms around her mother. "Mum," she said. "Why should Dad have to relax after his day? Why don't you have to relax after yours?" They clung to each other.

Brew came in and said he had the canapé tray in his hands and any time the two women wanted to quit the feminist boob bumping and come out and join the men the men would be glad. Oh, Oh, wait a second," he added with a sharp grin over at Kimberly. "I don't mean 'glad.' I mean 'feel good about it' and once we were able to have a toast to Grandma and we get a swallow of martini, you know, what, Kim, we will feel our 'concerns had been addressed.'"

"O Christ," said Kimberly, but she and her mother followed him out. "If this family would quit picking on me for using psychology management language and pick on Dad instead for harming a) American youth with his depraved TV sponsorships and b) harming the air, the water, and the ground of our planet, at least what's fucking left of it, then we would be talking about serious things."

"O dear, not again, darling," cried Barbara, a little loudly since she was coming along behind her daughter.

"Not again what?" cried Allison? "Barb, yours with olive. Without, Kim. Whisky with ice only, Brew, and Grandma, you've got yours."

"Hurray!" cried Persis, the grandmother." "We're all here! How wonderful!"

They sat and listened to two cardinals in their usual fir tree, and beyond them their American neighbors sounding jolly. It was Saturday evening. There were as many reasons to sound jolly as at any other particular time.

Allison stretched out, feet up on his chaise lounge, and looked over at his bright-eyed and beautifully stuck together mother. "Tell us about our school," he said leisurely.

They had all gone to the same school, Phillips Academy, usually just called Andover, or P.A. Even Brewster, the youngest, had gone, although some bequests and other favors were done, everyone knew, at the time of Brew's very late Placement.

Then he had done badly all 3 years he was there. He had done so poorly that he had not made it into any of five colleges he was allowed to put in for, so the family had met on it and decided he should work a year, then tutor, and try again. The family, in this case was really just Barbara. She had asked Allison to speak to whomever he ought to speak to about getting Brew into Yale. He had been needlessly crisp about it. "That's past my capabilities," he said. "Nothing's going to get Brew into anywhere. I think he should learn a trade, though, now I think about it, I'm not sure he could actually learn a trade. How would you like Brew to be the one to repair your Audi computer the day the whole car came to a stop on the Route 9? Forget it, sweetheart."

Barbara had said, "I know you are angry but you could go a little easier on Brew."

Allison had returned, "How do you mean, go a little easier? I get him into a kind of wonderful school and he never cracks a book the whole 3 years and now you want me to try to get Yale to think he's just swell and they should take him? Might as well ask a surgical patient to let a dope addict operate on him. Barb, the boy's a wastrel pure and simple. Reality check, Barb!"

She said, "OK, but we've never had a kid just drop out of everything that gives our life meaning."

It was that particular remark, made some months ago, when Kimberly had been home for Easter break, that started the most recent quarrel before this evening's fight.

"Now Mother," Kimberly had cut across the room with, "What would this 'everything' be that you say gives our life meaning. And whose life does it give all that meaning to? Am I included in this? I don't feel included."

Barbara said, "We've all gotten good educations. We speak a foreign language or two. We've read literature. You've even read some psychology. We're educated. So we're leaders. We have responsibilities in our community and we take them seriously. You know all this, Kim: why must you be so bad tempered about it?"

"Dad's not a leader. You know that, Mum."

"Of course he is!" The older woman snapped. "Who else runs everything around here from the tennis club to the symphony fund raising may I ask? Never mind being top man in his own considerable firm!"

"Dad's a follower, Mum," said Kim. "Whatever his classmates in school and college, and whatever his colleagues at the Company think is right, whatever his opposite numbers at those other companies thinks is right he glides right along with it. Dad slips along on every piece of corporate crap thinking and crap behavior that any USA firm can make a profit off."

Barbara said, "I won't be spoken to in this kind of language, Kimberly, really I won't. And I deeply resent those remarks about Dad. If it weren't for him this town would still keep blacks off all private tennis courts—and as for the condition of the courts themselves, if Daddy hadn't organized some people who know how to get things done, they'd still be clay with divots."

We needn't repeat the rest of that Easter break quarrel because it proceeded just exactly where such arguments go between steady, conservative parents and their rebellious college-age kids. Any middle-aged parent has been there and bought that same old same old hairshirt of a T-shirt. It is always the same. The change-agent kid decides the well-fixed parents should vote Democratic rather than Republican so that their tax dollars go to schools, social services, national health schemes, poverty-removal generally, instead of to tax counsel for depletion allowances in Texas oil, or worst of all, for USA hobby wars started up by old school classmates.

Parents respond in various ways. Not-so-smooth parents reply with, "Yes, well, if you would like to move out of the house and quit the school, I will contribute the $28,000 p.a. that the school costs me, to the poor, and you can get an apartment that's affordable with whatever wage you can earn after high-school hours, and still have some left over to contribute to the DNC, and Mom and I will always want you to come here for dinner as often as you're willing." That would be the message from the not-so-smooth parents. More punctilious parents would keep money out of it. "Look, son, look, daughter, I love it that you are going through this idealistic stage. I love it. It means you have a heart and you have enough moral imagination to know that the world suffers a lot—a lot—even if Mom and I have gone to some trouble to keep some of that suffering away from you yourself. That suffering of the world's—the poor, the helpless—it just isn't ever going to change, but maybe later in life, you'll remember these feelings you're having now, and you will say to yourself, I want to *pay back* for some of the privilege I've enjoyed all my life. And we both hope you do. You can't change the way the world is, but you can make small patches now and then. I'm proud you are my kid—caring the way you do."

That was the more statesmanlike parent speaking. The irony is, however, that the very hopelessness reiterated by that most loving parent instigates two unfortunate psychological dynamics for the young person:

1. That hopelessness (you can't bring about justice—you can only make small patches) teaches the poor won't ever get mercy and justice with any critical mass to it. The poor go on acting like poor people and therefore go on being poor. Bad luck, but there it is. And the rich go on networking with the rich and get richer.

2. The second psychological dynamic in that gentle-spoken parent's speech about hopelessness is that it is *usually* by far the most *sophisticated* argument of any kind that the son or daughter has ever heard. It is graceful. It is friendly. It invites that kid to return to filial respect and affection, as soon as they get over the aberrant stage. It gives that kid the golden arm, praising his or her idealism—and it shortens the months or years of that kid's *wanting* to be a change agent. In a word: it both welcomes that kid back into the graceful rhetoric of the rich *and* it gives permission to quit standing alone for principles.

But the family in our story here, Allison and Barb Goodnow,

Allison's mother, Persis, and the two fairly grown children, Kimberly and Brewster, have one major difference from the scenario described above. In that scenario, what Dad or Mom said, is *by far the most sophisticated argument that kid has ever heard.* In the Goodnow family nothing that either Barbara or Allison could say to Kimberly would even begin to be so sophisticated as what Kimberly has been hearing because Kimberly has been studying modern social psychology. She already learnt, at 19, some dynamics about why people do what they do—dynamics about why even educated and civil people, once in their daily *groups*, hatch up more ethically retro projects than do the lions and wolves or other pack-hunters of our planet.

We are reminded of Professor Ball's passage:

In the eyes (of our distant descendants) we are, or were, terrorists of a peculiarly savage stripe. Now let us imagine that historians in the 25th century want to know how their ostensibly civilized 20th and 21st century ancestors came to think and act in ways that are so savage and so destructive of their descendants' health, safety, and well-being.

The most wide-spread evil is brought about by organized groups of privileged people—those in commerce, those in government, and those in their high-tech armies. These groups are the people of a "peculiarly savage stripe" who Dr. Ball tells us will confound our descendants.

Therefore, we want to imagine some psychological dynamics that operate in such lucky leaders. We listen to the Goodnow family. We will look at the list that their mouthy daughter Kimberly brings along to the family happy hour to irritate her parents with. We will pay a little attention to the grandmother, because she has noticed, at exactly age 78—at her 60th class reunion at a good-old-school—that people kept using the phrase "I kind of want to *pay back*... now I am retired." We will give a quick lesson in how to find out others' hearts' truths by what is called "empathic inquiry." We will suggest that one can use that same "empathic inquiry" tool to find out hearts' truths that may be well hidden inside or under the conventional, pragmatic mindsets of people like Allison Goodnow. We need to think of Allison and Barbara's conscious beliefs and talk as the "majority voice" of their personalities. They each have a minority voice, as well; we will use empathic inquiry to learn it and to help Allison and Barbara to hear and feel respectful of that minority voice that lives hooded in their own personalities. How odd it sounds to say that the greatest single tool of moral imagination ever thought up so far—empathic inquiry—is the best single means of moral change *in adults*.

(Kimberly's sophomore course spread won't have given her any training in how to make a man in his fifties like her dad, or a woman in her fifties like her mother, decide that they will introduce constraint in avarice into their company life or into the actual pyramid of Allison's subsidiaries.)

We will describe a *second*, most important step of moral change: deciding to take it on, whatever the cost. Well—and what *would* be some of the costs? One might lose one's corporate position. One might lose one's "credibility" in the outlying environs of the corporate world. One might find one wasn't put up for some club. One might find (poor Allison! If he broke down and at last *did* try to get Brewster into some private college of decent standing) that one's friends don't seem to make the calls to college admissions deans the way they seemed to in the past. They might not remember to run it past Chet or Judith in the Athletic Department of whatever the college, that Al Goodnow, a nice guy in Massachusetts, even though his own son isn't a puck man at all, might be interested in springing for a complete new set of hockey equipment—well, that would be, if that kid got in to that college. Things like that could happen to a corporate leader and his or her spouse.

Sounds bad enough, worse to Barbara than to Allison because she was once outside the privileged loop. Still, here is something that *wouldn't* then happen to the Allisons and Barbaras of the United States. They would *not* make it the *entire* way to their graves without having put out for their best instincts. When they die, they won't have to say, I wish I had had a shot at the *Big* Virtues—rather than just the little manageable ones—local tennis court surfaces—and the unproblematic virtues, like supporting the

Boston Symphony. Nobody will ever reach for your throat just because you supported the Friends of the Symphony. If Allison and Barbara would try to reform their corporation, they would have taken on the biggest possible kind of work of goodness. Usually, however, when corporate people wake up to how exasperated and even heart-broken they are with the lying and the deceiving and the avarice of an American corporation, they don't try to reform it. They leave it. They don't think there exist any tools for making any one sizable corporation clean up its act because it is so tightly webbed with other corporations. What this does to a significant enclave of Americans, then, is leech principled people out of the corporations completely, leaving behind affluent, competent business people who are not proud of themselves. The psychoanalyst Viktor Frankl, wrote a very personable but no-nonsense book about this over a half-century ago: *Modern Man in Search of a Soul.*[1]

No such talk will take place on the Goodnows' terrace, however, because Allison has asked Persis to regale them with reunion stories.

"Come on, Mom," he said genially, grinning in his usual, friendly way, also looking, as always, tired and confident. "Give us the lowdown on our alma mater now!"

Everyone settled comfortably to listen to their nice grandmother, who, Kimberly had tactlessly explained earlier, has more joie de vivre than all the rest of the pack put together. No one objected much to Kimberly's statement that time, except that Barbara said she needn't to have referred to the family as "the pack." "We are not a bunch of wolves you know."

Now Persis told them that her class, being the 60-year class, got great treatment this time. Now that they were one of Andover's "Old Guard" classes, they found chairs set out for them in the grateful shade of the lawns. Between the talks and banquets of any reunion, before the final parade, old friends sat and ambled about, catching up with one another's family news. "I've noticed,"

---

1 Viktor Frankl, *Modern Man in Search of a Soul.*

Persis said, "It gets harder and harder to talk any kind of political issues or anything like that because now we are so old half of us don't care any more. People just get to their creaking feet and wander off looking distracted. Or right in the middle of a good conversation about gardens, someone mentioned a blood regimen they were on, and four others interrupted the people talking to bring out their dapper little pill packets to show. And then, worse, those who do care about civic life still have got polarized. The conservatives have gotten more conservative. The liberals have become positive screamers. So unless you're up for a lot of passionate outbreaks *those* conversations can be a drag.

"Way to go, idealistic liberals, if you ask me!" cried Kimberly. Her brother advised her that actually nobody *had* asked her.

The grandmother said hurriedly in a rising voice, "Oh, something else I was going to tell you guys." This was a liberal-arts-educated family so their idea of communication skills in an ugly moment was *to change the subject.* "I was going to tell you guys anyway," Persis said. "What you just said, Kimberly, about *idealists* reminds me. You know an odd thing that happened at this reunion that I don't remember hearing at *all* at my fiftieth: there we all were, sitting under the trees looking at the wonderful buildings, and some brave types—not me—being gallant about going up those stairs to look at upper-middler and senior students' artwork they had hung in the Addison Gallery. Over and over I heard different people saying the same thing: 'I want to *pay back*, somehow.' So I finally got to asking people, What do you mean with that 'pay back'? They always said, muttering some, that basically they meant pay back for their lifelong privilege and all."

"So I began to think about it. If a person feels they have to *pay back*, they must have taken something they shouldn't have taken. Or something they didn't pay the right price for in the first place."

"Way to go, Grandma!" cried Kimberly. She jumped up, went over, and gave old Persis a hug. "Oh, way to go, Grandma!"

But the old lady gave her only a brief smile. She had her

mind on something. "So you know what struck me," she went on, "what is it we fail to do in life that we should do? So why do we feel we have to *pay back*, so to speak, in *any* sense of the word?"

Kimberly had retaken her seat. "That's not a hard one, Grandma. We join into huge organizations—corporations, say— or even in smaller ones that can't make it unless they suck up to the larger ones. And then we do stuff at work, all the rest of our working lives, that sucks."

"Goddamn it, Kimberly" Allison remarked, but mildly.

Barbara said in a sharp voice: "You may use revolting language like that with your roommates, Kimberly! Please do us the favor of not using it here!"

"Yeah, right," said Brew, like the dormouse waking up at the mad tea party, "Spare us the gross language, Kimberly. You don't hear me coming off with a lot of doo doo language like that!" Once he had risen to the occasion that far, he appeared to recede into a daydream over his drink.

"Sorry, Mother," Kimberly said. "But you know, one of the things a psychology major learns is that people need *meaning* in their lives and that meaning seems to mean serious responsibility to the community. Otherwise, if people haven't got that sense of doing some sort of public good, they get neurotic."

Brew roused himself to say "Sounds like a pile of shit to me, actually."

Barbara instantly snapped, "And you can keep a clean tongue in your head, too, Brewy."

Allison sighed loud enough to carry through the pine trees to the neighbors in the next huge lot. "Well, Kimberly," he said, "Where is this conversation going, anyhow? If my nose doesn't deceive me, it smells as if it's coming back to the old round and round conversation about how Dad has been with his firm for thirty years and taken bonuses all that time, and bad old Dad sits on boards of other firms for which he is paid too much, and how very bad old Dad, despite shareholders' repeated proposals to the contrary, earns a lot more than twenty-five times the average of the whole company's salaries[2]. So of course Dad is a villain, who with his wife" —and here Allison reached across and grabbed the hand of Barbara that wasn't holding the chilled glass of martini—"yup, villain and loyal wife, who sprang for seven years' prep school and four years' college for their kids so far. Another four years of college, Brew, if you get into any college. Is that where this conversation is going?" He gave a non-sarcastic grin. "Going, er, again?"

Everyone looked at Kimberly. Her face now had that expression of languid expertise that college sophomores so often wear when home for holidays with their parents. Most parents know that look very well. That expression says: I am majoring in a new discipline that wasn't around when *you*, Dad, or *you*, Mom, went to college. Or worse it says: you could have taken psychology and ethics, Dad and Mom, but you didn't do it, did you?

Kimberly now had that look. Allison and Barbara held hands tighter and Barbara gave her martini a 180 cartwheel into her mouth and throat. It brought some color to her face. Both parents' unconsciously tipped their shoulders slightly toward each other. One loves one's kids a lot, the shoulders seemed to say, but in this kind of thing, one hangs close to the loyal spouse.

Kimberly now said, "You want to know what this is all really about, Dad? It's about your firm and other firms just all the time doing just as filthy stuff as they can get away with. No——Dad! Dad!—hear me out. Your company is an aggregate that owns other companies selling bad stuff to kids whose parents aren't educated enough to have a clue how bad the stuff is. You know that. Two of those companies under your company make zillions and zillions selling sweet pops, still with carcinogenic ingredients, although they *know* they are carcinogenic, never mind the carbon-

---

2 Most corporations publish in their Annual Reports a very few of the many shareholder proposals they receive during a year. Despite that, one can't help noticing that shareholders repeatedly ask for less discrepancy between top officers' compensation and average management and workers' compensation by the firm. A common request is the one Allison's referring to: a stockholder request that top officers' not get more than 25 times the average for everybody on the firm's payroll. The Board of Directors without exception reject such proposals, almost without exception giving the reason that if they so delimited what top staff get they won't be able to attract top talent. The idea of most shareholders is that satisfaction of the implied avarice wouldn't necessarily get the "top talent."

ation which damages the kidneys, never mind the sugar-addiction aspect of it, never mind the aspartame, which is a killer. And who buys that addictive stuff and drinks it? The uneducated poor and uneducated lower middle class—and why: because no one tells them not to. Which ghetto parent or which overworked laboring parent or which hard-pressed small-salaried support-staff parent or delivery-boy parent is on the web accessing the truth about the shit in the pop that you, Dad, and your friends, sell them? Really, Dad. You guys are like Reynolds Tobacco. Kill everyone with cancer, if there's money in it, and your lawyers are good enough to hold off the Fed. Charming." Now Barbara let loose Allison's hand. She leaned forward.

"Hold it, Mom," Kimberly said. "Then you get your chance."

Her younger brother still lay half-sprawled on the flower-printed cushions of his lawn lounge chair. His eyes were now open all the way, though, and he kept them steady on his sister. She noted to herself how infuriating that was. Brew must have read somewhere that you should have eye-contact, hey, but she could tell he was just trying to look interested. Or maybe he'd poured himself something extra on his last trip into the pantry and was having a civilized little drunk by himself. Or he was just waiting her out, looking polite and interested, until he himself could put in some remark. Kimberly thought to herself, what a lazy creep Brewy really was, but she made her mind stay on task here. She gathered up her family in her slow, turning gaze. She included Grandma, who was now sitting upright like the Parthenon. Way to go, Grandma, Kimberly thought.

Aloud she said, "Dad, your company doesn't even try to find out what ethical behavior might mean. You don't even try. *No, wait, Dad,*" she said. "Those ethics conferences that you haul in from time to time. You know perfectly well that no one with two brain cells to rub together would sit through one of those things if they could get out of it, with those dumbfake psychologists telling people to imagine they are on a warm beach. All that suck stuff for your lowest-paid staff. And what are these low-paid staff supposed to do after a half-day of imagining they are on a warm beach and all? They are supposed to vent *off* whatever bothers them about their supervisors, and then feel better, and then go back to work thinking they work for one hell of a caring firm. Meanwhile, their kids go to USA public schools with the social workers being fired because the USA rich want that salary money for industrial war contracts. Those lowest-paid staff members' kids sit in classrooms with so many other kids in them it isn't a teaching situation. It's a crowd management situation. Dad—Mom—let me tell you, it isn't a *teaching* situation. I did some field trips and I *know.* Mom, going to Dobbs was such a big deal in your life. Did you ever, as in even once, sit in a classroom at Dobbs with fifty people in it trying to understand a piece of math or literature? How about 70 people? Did it ever occur to you that we could change the *public* schools so that people—teacher and kids— could think together? The way we got to at Andover?"

Brew had discreetly taken over his dad's job of stirring and pouring refills.

Kimberly now said, "OK, only one more thing. You guys, Dad especially, but you, too, Mom—you're always talking about loyalty. Loyalty. Family solidarity. More loyalty. All that loyalty is loyalty to *your friends.* Friends who make money in the same really unscrupulous ways you guys are so good at. How about loyalty to the United States with its poor?"

Now Barbara had stood up, her face fully the color of blood. She was lighted with fury.

"Please, Mom," Kimberly said. "If you are about to recite again that one stanza that every Republican seems to know by heart about how if you're at a B & B for a weekend near Dover Beach, the two of you should be true to one another because otherwise all there is is ignorant armies clashing in the night? Those ignorant armies clashing in the night, Mom: let me just ask you: who makes all the defense contract money off those ignorant armies when they get to doing their clashing? That's the USA foreign policy, with huge companies like Dad's getting together to raise the huge money-making contracts that you say your shareholders want you to get. Actually, Mom, and Dad, I am a shareholder in your company, and I object."

Silence lay over the terrace. Everyone's glass was blessed with seconds. From the pantry, which stood between the kitchen and the dining area, well behind the open French doors, came a roseate scent of flank steak now done. Crusted onto its surface and stuck in all over at knife point, rosemary, garlic and wine turned the June night as redolent as Christmas. No one spoke.

Barbara presently got to her feet. "I'll just check…" she said, as she went woodenly into the house.

The grandmother suddenly said, "Kimberly…" The old woman's voice was not that strength that it'd once been—as Tennyson said about Odysseus, and old Persis often said about herself, with a good-natured laugh. Her voice timbre was light these last years, and she sometimes had to catch a fresh breath before finishing a sentence. But now she sent her speech sailing like a clear silver ray across to her granddaughter. "Business has always made money any way it could, so long as it didn't get into too much trouble. Kimberly, you can't change that. It's human nature. Some things just *are*, dear Kimmy. You can't teach a cat not to catch mice."

Everyone except Kimberly smiled.

Kimberly said, "Like slavery, Grandma? Slavery is human nature. There was always slavery, and everyone said you couldn't change it but one day in 1863 it wasn't legal any more in the United States. And child labor, Grandma. Child labor is human nature. Everyone had it, and then one day in 1895 we didn't have it any more. All the bad things are human nature. But some human beings sometimes cut through some of the bad things."

Now her kid brother roused himself. He called across to Kimberly, "Yeah, Kimberly hey. Commercial polluting goes way back, too. In the middle ages the sheep tanning people were pol-luting rivers with tannic acid."

Allison glanced over gratefully, the way one does when just anybody heaves really just any fresh note into a stale conversation.

Brewster said, "So this group of English people from down-stream came up to tell them that the tannic acid was wrecking their drinking water. 'Is that right?' The sheep processors said. 'How many are you chaps down there, anyhow?' They felt puzzled but they estimated, fifty, seventy-five, whatever the figure was. So the sheep processors hired some thugs. One night they went along the towpath downstream and beat up on the males of those villagers. No more complaints after that."

Barbara had now returned and was hovering. Dinner was ready.

"I don't believe that story for one moment," she told Brewster.

He got up, and gave his grandmother an arm. They started in to dinner. "I didn't think you would, Mom, but if it makes it any easier for you, you know that little weirdo P.A. classmate of mine you always cottoned to so much? The one who got into an OK college and wasn't it a shame that our Brewy had failed us etc, etc, Mom, You remember? Well *he* got that story out of a freshman econ course at Wesleyan. I'll get you the book."

Grandma went along on Brewster's arm. They were slow, because of her horrible knee, but formal, like people in a parade. "Those old classmates of mine," she said, turning around to address Allison and Kimberly who were coming along behind: "Maybe they were doing all the bad stuff Kimberly says your company does, Allison. Maybe *that's* the sort of stuff they want to *pay back* for."

The little group took turns at the sideboard. The smell of Barbara's always wonderful cooking cheered them. They realized they loved one another.

Gradually, gradually, they all pulled together. Barbara had done them proud and they knew it. She had 1.5 maids to do the cleaning. She got a green card for one of them and stiffed an Immigration officer on behalf of the other. An occasional man came around to shovel snow off their walks in winter, and an old man whom Allison liked to chew the fat with because he had lived in the town before it became a suburb, trimmed their oaks and stapled down the sister-plants in their strawberry patch. But Barbara herself did all the cooking. All of her married life she paid attention to it. She never just fried something any how. The green beans tonight, with their tiny cubes of red peppers tossed in, were actually fragrant. She had taken the trouble to bring home two bunches of flowers, most beautifully out of season. The kids were home. The kids were home.

"You've done it again, Barb," said her mother-in-law, passing with a handsomely filled plate.

But angels and serpents have one thing in common. Say we saw a viper ease itself over our doorsill and into our house—say everyone saw it slither in there, not necessarily into the nursery, but somewhere in there, and everyone knew it hadn't come back out. The family of that household would feel edgy. They might deny the snake's presence, but they each know it is in there somewhere. The same with the presence of angels in the house— say the angel is a new moral idea—once we know that a new, unasked-for but undeniably genuine, moral idea comes into the house, people feel edgy.

It won't spoil their appetite or gratitude for Barbara's cooking. They each thank her extra heartily. Goll darn but she does well by them! They keep saying that kind of thing, sometimes with their mouths full. Her mother-in-law can keep saying, "You've done it again, Barb!" and she says it all over again at dessert because Barbara Goodnow is one of about six American family cooks who knows a trifle has to be 98% saturated with liquor and the custard part has to be real custard, not vanilla Jell-O mix and especially not just whipping cream. And Allison can go around with the sauterne topping up for everyone. Despite all that, they all feel the presence of the new moral expectation. It nearly palpably glides among them. They feel the way they felt the first Christmas Eve after an adult came clean to them about Santa Claus. You pretend that everything's the same. You pretend you don't care and that Christmas will be the same, but it doesn't feel the same. And why isn't it the same? Because you are no longer an entitled little kid with a right to magical presents.

After the dishwasher had been set to growling and hissing over its first load, Barbara realized she was mad.

She knocked on Kimberly's door and went in at the "Come

in!" She perched on the edge of Kimberly's bed.

Kimberly sat at her desk, wearing glasses instead of the usual contacts, looking older and wise. My dear daughter, Barbara thought, half seeing Kimberly ahead by 30 or 40 years, an old wise woman, when all Barbara wanted was that her beautiful Kimberly would get to stay young forever.

Then Barbara's anger returned to her.

"We have to talk," she brought out. "I wonder if you realize that Daddy has forgotten more than you've ever learned in the first place. You come home from college and berate us all, and you're nineteen years old. You forget, darling, we have all been to school and college."

Kimberly gave her a very nice full smile but she didn't leave her desk. She looked down at her mother, pen still in hand.

Barbara can't make out individual words that Kimberly is writing, but clearly she is writing a list in two columns, justified at the left.

"It's very, very hard on Daddy, darling," the mother said. "Your talk like that about his work and the company. The company's a large part of his life; surely you know that."

Kimberly said, "Daddy needs to shape up, actually, Mom."

Barbara flung out both hands. "Who says? Why do kids always think the *parents* have to shape up? How about you and Brew shaping up? I don't hear much about that!"

The two women got sidetracked onto Brewster for a while. Apparently, while Kimberly was away for this last semester, Brew had begged his father to pull some strings and somehow get him into Yale. He'd had the gall to name even the college he wanted. Davenport, Dad, he'd apparently said, Davenport College, he meant, if you could swing it, Dad.

That stupid clot, thought Kimberly. She let her mother tell the story. Her mother went on talking about how Allison ought to do something for Brew or he would be knocked out of everything that mattered.

Kimberly cut in and said, "What's everything 'that matters,' Mom?"

Barbara looked savage. "You know as well as I do. Well—not quite as well. You haven't *been there*—in the life *without* all this—and I have."

Kimberly restrained herself. She took up a careful, non-aggressive tone. "Look, Mom, you know I'm glad someone put you in touch with someone who knew someone and they drove you over to somewhere to take the Placement Tests for Independent Schools. And you got into Dobbs Ferry. I'm glad, Mom. But can't you say to yourself how wonderful it would be if *all* American kids could get an education in small classrooms like that? You never had to sit in rooms with 70 kids jammed in it. Don't you want the others to escape, too?"

But Barbara had got to her feet.

"You had better get hold of some sense of the real world, darling," she said. "You can't change these things. You just can't. If you keep trying to change everything you're going to become a screamer and a very shrill young lady and then no—"

Kimberly cut in. "Let's see if I can guess, Mom. No man with any decent prospects will want to marry me? Is that what you were saying, Mom? Were you going to say that?"

Barbara brought her lips together. She seemed to look out from between her eyeliner like a knight out from his narrow vizor.

"Mom, isn't that what Republican parents tell their daughters? If you get idealistic you'll be unattractive and then you won't be able to get a rich husband? The way they tell their sons if you get idealistic you'll look a fool and get eased out of all the loops where the money is?"

Barbara turned, at the door, and said, "You do a lot of talking for someone whose semester worksheets are met by her dad twice a year!"

Kimberly paused and then said, "Mom, you weren't going to say that since Dad pays for everything I should keep my mouth shut, were you, Mom? Were you going to say that, Mom?"

Barbara Goodnow burst into tears and fled the room.

The daughter swiveled her chair around and looked at her

list. It wasn't only a list. At the top she had done a paragraph
that said:

Dear Dad, I have been thinking of a list you could make. Then
after you had the list actually written down, with PEOPLE AND
OTHER CREATURES WHOM WE HAVE BEEN HARMING at the
top—not just "Concerns we all have" or some other shit language
like that—verbatim write *People and Other Creatures We Have
Been Harming.* Then make a list of the ways in which your company and those under you have been harming people or animals
or earth and water, and so on. Here is the list I have, but I have
just read your annual reports and webpages and my econ texts.
You will know better.

1. Psychological stunting to children and youth via violent TV
programming.

2. Psychological damage to youth through comic TV programming in which idealists, thinkers, and anyone not crowd-adapted
are made fun of.

3. Advertisements that constantly implicitly or explicitly tell
people that happiness comes of high-income kinds of recreation
expenditure.

4. Financing the campaigns of Senators and Representatives
who will agree to mine needed moneys from the education and
social services, from all helping service delivery, in order to pay
for industrial weaponry contracts.

5. Producing food products that poison kids and adults alike
with chemical additives.

At the bottom, Kimberly wrote: Dad, I have left out all the eco-
logical damage your ring of companies does because you have
been litigated against so often about them that you know what the
cases are.

Then she returned to the list itself and wrote at the bottom of
the Victims column at right, All of us, Dad. All of us. Not just the
poisonous sweet "juices" that the poor are told are good for their
kids. Not just the violent TV. It's the lying, Dad. To read your company's website you'd think you guys were seriously helping local
communities everywhere you have a plant. Then we find out that

all that "Good Citizen of the Year Award" stuff is just whitewashing over your carrying on your harmful products-and-services deliveries. The lying makes us all feel cynical. All of us.

Then, to her own surprise, the enterprising Kimberly put her head down in her hands and wept.

We leave the Goodnow family here. Because of the corporate culture they come from, none of them, not even the ambitious, hard-thinking Kimberly, knows anything about two 1990s philosophies that could be linked together to change the "peculiarly savage stripe" of American businesses.

Let us brace ourselves for a second not to sneer, but to consider this: there really are, out there, in the hands of some neurologists and some educators and some helping professionals two philosophies, which, if top-level people in corporations were to learn them, and use the one as a psychological tool for the other, might help them build the *will to constrain themselves and their group* from the current depredations on others and despoiling of the earth. The first is the biological and philosophical and psychological principle of *stage development*.

And what exactly is "stage development philosophy" that it is the warmly welcomed baby of modern neurobiologists and psychologists? (Philosophers have always liked stage-development theory, but they haven't had in their hands scientific researches of a kind to support their ideas.)

It is important to realize that the ordinary corporate and liberal-arts academic worlds have just gone along with the old typologies because no one told them that the Myers-Briggs delineations are a farce of an especially static-thinking sort. No one has told corporate human resources people to look seriously into modern-day stage-developmentalists.

Every time a corporation runs some of its job applicants or its people already hired through a Myers-Briggs or a look-alike to see what "types" people are, that corporation is implicitly saying human beings come in types. Since the findings of 1990s neurology and especially 1995-2003 neurology absolutely dispatches that old-fashioned, bizarre, static, and reductive thinking—taking people for types at all—it does us all a disservice that corporations keep re-pointing that outdated wall that needs to tumble down. Stage development theory, on the contrary, has myriad sources, in ancient times from philosophers, more recently from the sciences and from economic theories, and most recently from psychologists. Some of these stage-developmentalists' names are famous— Aristotle to the extent that he addresses ethical *development*; Friedrich Schiller (yes, oddly enough); Adam Smith, yes, but only where he is *talking* development. Most recently and better known for just this: Jean Piaget, Erik Erikson, Henry Sullivan, Lawrence Kohlberg, Jane Loevinger, to name a few. The idea is this: as even the tiniest of entities moves and chooses how to move next, it changes. Just as someone who has acted merely pratically but now decides to curb some of his or her aggression or avarice, let us say, changes. Function recreates an entity as it lives out its life. This idea, usually stuffily referred to as dynamic functionality, is the most freedom-giving aspect of ethical stage-development theory. Stage-developmentalists tend to admire their own specific theory more than they admire others' theories, so they make quarrelsome remarks about their colleagues or opposite numbers—but actually all of them share certain philosophical assumptions that make us a) believe that our ideas of goodness are not just cultural riff, but a deep potential of our species. And b) all of them say the news is good: when you let a human being be treated with maximum respectful love, directive leadership when young, inviting that human being to a sense of humor about life—not kidding, mind you—but the kind of humor that comes of philosophical perspective—then the result will not be someone depending on violence for kicks, sadism for sexual pleasure, or in things governmental, war to break up the ennui.

Roughly speaking: nearly all stage-development theories suggest five or six levels of ethical outlook possible for people. (We say *possible*, since sociopaths are people stuck at Stage 1 for decades. And a good many black-and-white thinkers are stuck at Stage 2 for decades. Millions are stuck all their lives at stage 3.) But originally the mind, if treated properly especially when young, has the potential for these six stages and scientists have watched and made studies.

The first stage is total selfishness. One wants what one wants and one constrains oneself for no person or no reason. This stage is appropriate for babies who must howl in order to get fed and to keep people sheltering them.

The second stage outlook is that one prefers one's own tribe, one's own church, one's own government. These preferences are serious, not just a matter of taste. One's own group is *right*: the other is either *wrong* or they are just outlying resources. They aren't real to us. If we are in stage 2 we practice shameless colonialism. On our own children, too. Dr. Terence Ball's essay cited on the first page explains ethics as loving and respecting not only what is ours, close up, but what is farther away—indeed, farther away in time as well as space. That is, it is not only not OK to bomb people outside one's own country, it is not OK to grab global resources which will be needed by people alive generations from now. Second stage persons, however, are much like fundamentalist churchpersons: what is *we, us, ours, is good and we will die on the field of battle to preserve it.* Whatever is they is either unclear to us, or it is adjudged to be wrong-minded. A stage 2 person often finds it a moral necessity to kill some of those others.

The third stage is one in which we decide what is good or bad and how we should be and behave in the universe by looking at our colleagues or confreres—or, most typically, the other teenagers in our peer group.

One reason that corporate leaders are so ignorant and what's more, scornful of, psychology is that the corporate leaders they know are ignorant and scornful of psychology. They do not study neuroscience, even though it may well be the most exciting and freedom-saving of all fields of knowledge in the early 2000s. Liberal-arts educated people and engineering people are in large part ignorant of moral psychology. They hate the jargon from what little they've heard of it, too—which keeps them from welcoming a few texts about group psychology into their thinking. Allison Goodnow, now in his fifties, will fight off any idea that people in his class generally do fight off. Barbara, who struggled to get out of working-class America, and joyfully landed in very, very upper-class America, is certainly not going to look into fields of philosophy that her now-peers would jeer at. She is in the inner circle and staying there is a much greater passion for her than discovering new doors to altruism.

In the fourth stage, one is obedient to the authorities and the conventions of one's class—its ideas of what is honorable and what is not. An example: one serves one's country. One does not allow attacks on it. The class that Allison and Barbara Goodnow belong to, to give an example, admires dutifully promised and fulfilled civic work in beauty—beauty in tennis courts, city streets, the Boston Symphony, libraries. It admires doing work well. It despises the efforts of people to change the system. It admires the beauty of the Andover campus and it admires the small classes at The Masters School at Dobbs Ferry, but Allison and Barbara's class leaders long ago decided that legislators who would like to make America's public schools into Andover or Dobbs for ordinary kids are out of their minds. Their parents and grandparents taught them such idealism is simply unrealistic and they will teach that hopelessness to their children as well. They will teach it like gentlemen and gentlewoman perhaps—gravely, showing their children they feel sad about it—but giving no quarter. No monies go to bring beautiful campuses or Socratean conversation to public schools. A nutty idea. Stage 4 people, given their fealty to class conventions, can barely hear the Kimberly Goodnows when they speak out.

A fifth stage person thinks for himself or herself, deliberately trying to look at things not as the neighbors look at them, not as their own background announces they *ought* to look at them. Stage 5 is about individual idealism. And usually the fifth-stage person *is* an idealist, not merely a pragmatic ego-centered go-getter. Oddly enough, the later moral stages are more altruistic and more uncontaminated by public opinion than the earlier ones.

Most moral-development schemes have six stages. In the sixth stage a person's relationship to the universe is affectionate and humble. One has the feeling that all beings are related, and that a kind of brotherhood or sisterhood is possible if only we would keep it in mind. Stage 6 people are not all goodness and light, though. They almost uniformly hold a resounding hatred of fundamentalist religions of any kind. They not only admire formal and conceptual thinking: they tend to look down their noses at concrete, limited, anecdote-ridden thinking. They want to have a world philosophy in which whatever is pleasant and engaging to oneself is made and kept possible for all other creatures as well.

We said that there were two philosophy-based practices that the corporate culture is ignorant of. Any philosophy can be described as a psychological condition, as scholars often and usefully do[3]. One of these is in not one, but two, ways interesting with respect to moving our corporate leader from obdurate pragmatism to moral imagination. It is empathic inquiry. When young people are treated to regular empathic inquiry by their elders, they move out of the coarser ethical stages described above *faster* than if they were ignored or jeered at. Lawrence Kohlberg, in his *The Philosophy of Moral Development: Moral Stages and the Idea of Justice*, Vol. 1, *Essays on Moral Development*[4] pointed out that middle-class children seemed to reach higher stages faster than did Central American village children not because they were of better stock or anything like that, but because there were more empathic conversations in their families. If we think back to the easy way in which the Goodnow family talked to each other, even when chiding, even when quarreling outright, we can see that the senior Goodnows are not giving their children a peasant life. Kimberly and Brewster had the ear of Allison and Barbara. Allison and Barbara had the ear of Persis. Everyone's remarks were responded to.

Empathy, a word we are all sick to death of while most of us haven't an idea what it means, is a way of people paying attention to one another's ideas. Empathic questioning does not come natu-

---

3 See Daniel N. Robinson's *An Intellectual History of Psychology, Third edition*, and Tom Kitwood, *Concern for Others: A New Psychology of Conscience and Morality*.
4 Lawrence Kohlberg, *The Philosophy of Moral Development: Moral Stages and the Idea of Justice, Vol 1, Essays on Moral Development*, Harper and Row, San Francisco, 1981.

rally to people. They learn it the way a carpenter learns a skill. What comes naturally is contrived ways of communication that get people to yes as that famous manipulative book describes. What comes naturally is industrial psychology, when the conversation is made so frightening that the mark or dupe desists from some behavior that was not practical for the industrial psychologist who orchestrated their meeting. Empathic inquiry is quite opposite to such natural stage 1 or stage 2 conversations, because it always, by its definition, helps the person being empathized with to become *more clear and more committed to his or her own spirit.* This is not the good manners taught to State Department personnel to keep Consulate receptions neutral. Nor is it the hideous, dishonorable, kidding of upper class parents with their innocent children, in which the family party line says one must have a sense of humor about oneself, but it is really just bullying. One can make a test about how much sense of humor someone ought to have about himself or herself. Should Florence Nightingale have had a wry sense of humor about the needlessly sickened British common soldier being killed by regimental indifference?

Here is a basic format. It is very basic. It is very difficult to do if you've never done it.

A Five-Step Format for Basic Empathic Questioning[5]

The first step (often completely missed!) is deciding to hear our own thoughts or others' thoughts at all. Our usual, *merely natural* practice is this: someone starts talking, and, being nice people, we listen for a minute or two. Then we decide we know what he or she is saying, or "where they're coming from," so we quit listening. If we have good manners we let him or her go on talking, but in our hearts we are really just waiting for the other person to quit so *we* can talk.

The second step is emptying yourself of *your own point of view* or of any association of yours that comes to mind as the

---

5 This format is based upon the Five-Step Basic Empathic Questioning Format by Mary Peterson, LICSW, and Carol Bly, DHL, used for the Fall Ethics retreats of Shattuck-St Mary's School seniors, Faribault, Minnesota

speaker speaks.

Bad example No 1. Say the speaker says, "I had surgery on my hand last week." The response: "Yeah? My mother had hand surgery and it was the devil of a thing for weeks and weeks after that."

Bad example No. 2: the speaker says, "Jesus told a great story about an older son who got it OK about property *values* but didn't get it about love," to which the other person replies, "Yes, there have always been a lot of storytellers around. Buddha, too. He told stories a good four hundred years before Jesus did."

In both of these examples, the listeners rushed into contributing peripheral slants of their own instead of staying with whatever the speaker's underlying idea might turn out to be. The dullest human conversation is constructed this way—and good ideas get accidentally trampled by such random self-centeredness as the listener demonstrated.

Ask the person who just spoke, or yourself, if you are practicing empathy upon your self in order to see your own deeper take on this, some open-ended—not yes-or-no questions about *what he or she just said.* Most Americans have never once been asked to enlarge on or refine anything they have just said. Here is where we get a sense of how manipulative Socrates let himself be with those yes or no questions, designed half to help readers think, and half to show up the other speaker as inconsistent. *Empathy is nothing like Socratic questioning.* The usual aim of empathy at this third point is to collect further data from the speaker, further reported feeling, and further reported meaning that the speaker attaches to those data and feelings. Why? To help the speaker himself or herself pull up those data, pull up the feelings involved, and become conscious of the meaning he or she had attached to it all back then—now becoming conscious of it for the first time. What if Kimberly suspected that Allison and Barbara were really only 95% sure of their opinion that major moral *systemic* change is hopeless, that corporations must go on acting the way they act. What if they were 5% unsure—full of half-realized anxiety, full of a kind of disparate wretchedness. At least, prey to wistfulness. If

Kimberly had known how to ask them empathic questions about everything in that 5% of their feeling, they might come to see themselves differently. They might decide, what's more, that they were not 95% sure of their fatalism about corporate morality: they were only 50% sure. Empathic questioning wakes up the slumberous virtue in people more often than it wakes up some ugly brutal instinct. It wakes up the loyal opposition—the dissenting voice inside the toughest of us.

In Step 4 the questioner paraphrases what the speaker has just said, to make sure that what the speaker said (and the questioner duly heard) was the speaker's deepest, most exact meaning. After listening to the paraphrase, the speaker sometimes says, "Well, yes. You have it right all right. I did say that. But now I hear *you* saying it in your voice, I realize I don't really mean that. I thought I did but now I don't." Then the empathic questioner needs to ask, "So how does it go *now*—as far as you can tell".

Here is the part of the empathy format that few outside of social workers and existential therapists know about: it is that the empathic person helps the speaker to look *forward instead of backward*, and *to make tentative plans for the future*. The empathic questioner says something like, "OK. Given those data, feelings, and meanings that you've just reported, what do you see as a good direction for you to go from here? What might be the ideal goal? Or goals—maybe one for now and some long-range ones further out there?"

We have proposed that the best means of lessening the avarice of American corporations will involve getting acquainted with the very hopeful developmental theories coming out of not only 1990s and 2000s neuroscience but from psychologists and educators. Having that view—that people can grow, even in adult life—and then acquiring themselves the skill of empathic inquiry might free thousands and thousands of executives from their inherited rubric that ethical growth in business groups is mere St. Elmo's Fire. That rubric is like most privileged people's privilege—merely inherited. People recite it quite naturally, the way they recite psalms learned in childhood. It is always hard to give up any philosophy, such as hopelessness, if it goes back to earliest memory and if it is still voiced aloud by old friends and peers. Hard.

There is one psychological dynamic that will make it harder, however, for Allison and Barbara to give up their complacent passivity about what his corporation does. That is this: both of them, like nearly all privileged people, get to work most of their lives on projects that will *succeed.* Allison and Barbara, and Persis, too, when she was still doing community projects, always feel fairly sure of the outcome. That's why they ask their peers to give heavily to make sure Boston will always have major music. That is why they give, and ask peers to give, middle-sized capital help to public tennis facilities and the like. Not only will such projects always succeed but, no one will think badly of you when you engage in them. Such surety as the Goodnows feel, when they promptly fulfill their volunteer committee commitments and so on, is requisite and perfectly OK for mid-level virtues.

Yet the greatest work of humankind—moral change for the better, scientific research of the basic, intellectually demanding sort, all protest movements against debilitating practices of a government, and all ethical philosophy—all these greatest of human tasks are inevitably conducted in an atmosphere of likely failure— in an atmosphere not only of likely failure, however, but with feelings of being embattled. So these greatest tasks take place in an atmosphere of likely failure and resolute good humor and gratitude for any colleagues we can muster to the cause.

Allison and Barbara haven't really worked at goals with so much uncertainty. They would have to develop the psychological muscle to plug away despite the uncertainty. Still, these two are especially lucky because they are a talky family and talk keeps principles alive. Their greatest luck is that they have a daughter passionately interested in justice. She will cheer any reform they take on with a fresh shout of joy and surprise.

We described a smart, talkative family in hopes that lucky corporate predators, if any read this, will look around at their own families, not to see the loyal *group*—anyone can do that at any birthday party or funeral—but to ask themselves this: among my family here…are there some serious moral thinkers like Kimberly? And in myself, is there some voice in there, among my own various voices, that would like me to do better work in the world?

—Carol Bly and Cynthia Loveland

———————————— // ————————————

Afterword for non-Social Workers
and
Social Workers, too

Why would a professional Social Worker get mixed up in writing and publishing stories and essays?

What is a Social Worker anyway? People suppose they know. We get written off as naïve but idealistic do-gooders helping the poor. Or as nosey villains who remove innocent children from their families. Media plays a part in our picture of Social Workers. Most recently TV's Maxine Gray has been the model. Kindhearted, frazzled by overwork, she rushes in her clompy shoes to rescue children from harm. This portrayal has much truth to it: in fact, it is the most accurate TV portrayal I have seen of a child welfare worker. Still, it leaves out the distinctive concepts of the Social Work profession.

What is not generally known is that Social Work skills and knowledge are something very different from those of other helping professions.

Social Workers have to know not only a lot of psychology but a lot of sociology as well. Social Work, oddly enough, is the only helping profession that focuses on people not just as individuals but as members of groups. We all live our lives in connection with others, in families, in work groups, in social groups, in recreational groups, in neighborhood groups and even in spiritual groups. The people in our lives play a part in the decisions we make and in how we view the world. When working to help people heal and grow we take the social milieu into account. Doctors and teachers recognize the importance of the social environment to healing and learning but depend on us to know how to tie it together. That's why we're in hospitals and clinics and schools. Our understanding of the individual within his or her environment allows us to help people recognize particular psychological pressures that they will be up against from those around them when they are trying to make change.

Social Justice, our belief in it and our responsibility to work toward it, is a stalwart principle of Social Work. We believe that children need to be protected and that they have a right not only to safety but to affection and respect. And we believe that the poor are entitled to the basic necessities of life; food, shelter, medical care, not based on some system of merit but simply based on need. And we believe in basic justice for everyone— civil rights, an equitable piece of the American apple pie, the right to not be taken advantage of by those more rich or more powerful. Even the poor have the right to make their own decisions about their lives.

We believe the rich as well as the poor can change. But, we are also systems people. We believe societies can change and often should. We are always doing both—helping people deepen and helping harmful systems change.

Hopelessness is a four letter word to us. We're not the ones who hang up the trendy posters that tell people to *recognize what you can change and give up on the rest*. And we don't share the liberal arts view that it can be classy and sensible to write off certain causes as hopeless. That stance gives a person permission to quit before even starting. We know people can change, systems can change, and whole societies can change. We don't give up. We're particularly stubborn on this point.

In the United States, however, poor children and rich children regularly get taught hopelessness. The lesson is slightly different for each group but it goes something like this:

Four horrible notions that *poor* children get taught:
>Life will never be different.
>
>Fair doesn't exist
>
>It's no use trying to change things: the effort will just be wasted.
>
>It's ok to be angry but useless to turn that anger into action toward change.

Nor are rich children spared. Idealism in young privileged teens is typically seen as charming by their educated parents; those same parents, however, want their kids cured of societal idealism by the time they are 19 or 20—so they don't become gadflies to the status quo. We see the perfect case in Kimberly in the "The Savage Stripe."

So here's how hopelessness is taught to rich kids:

Four horrible notions that *rich* children get taught:
>The poor are poor and always will be so no use wasting time trying to change things.
>
>The poor probably brought the situation on themselves anyway; we aren't responsible.
>
>Failing to see or acknowledge the poor—pretending they don't exist—is a wise precaution against becoming pointlessly shrill.
>
>If the poor don't exist we don't have to feel any pain or discomfort when we do nothing.

A classic technique Social Workers use to help both groups and individuals deepen their thinking and feeling is empathic listening.

Empathic listening is completely different from conversational listening. In social conversation it is all right to listen just long enough to get the gist of what the speaker is saying or just long enough to be polite. It is all right to join in with our own story or our own take on the speaker's story. We can even change the subject completely. Social Workers, too, do this kind of listening to our friends and family: we are not always on the job! Empathic listening means listening for meaning and reflecting back to the speakers how we understood what they said. Empathic listening encourages speakers to clarify for us and themselves their own thoughts, perceptions, emotions and ideas. The focus stays with the speakers, who by hearing themselves out better recognize their own thoughts and feelings. We listen to the stories of our clients. We help them sort through. Sometimes they make new connections and see things differently. And sometimes they make amazing changes in both behavior and attitudes.

Listening to our *own* stories is something we can all learn to do. We can ask ourselves questions, and from that listening and questioning we can grow into our deeper selves.

In this same questioning way we can learn from the stories of others and even from the stories of great literature. Curiously, blessedly, we sometimes recognize lies that have been taught us along the way. Sometimes we can even manage to unlearn those lies.

Let me tell you a couple of lies I've managed to unlearn. The first is the lie that any *difference of opinion is a potential argument and argument is bad.* By this standard any "discussion" is potentially bad. At my childhood house all "controversial" topics were off limits. This prohibited politics, religion, current events, even much of literature. Odd, since my mother had been an English major and a librarian. All this because she couldn't stand dissent. Anyone can see how her terror might well stifle inquiry, prevent learning from the opinions of others or the testing out of our own ideas. Not to mention that it makes for very dull conversation.

The second lie that I have unlearned is that *appearance is more important than substance.* One example is still vivid. I was ten and my sister Jean was five. Jean had gone to vacation bible school. On the last day all the kids were promised popsicles before going home. The school ran out and Jean didn't get one. She cried. The kind minister's wife, Mrs. Heimarck, took pity on her and took her to Barnes Drug Store (our neighborhood store in SW Minneapolis), bought her a popsicle, and drove her home. Mrs. Heimarck explained it all to my mother who greeted her warmly and thanked her politely. As soon as Mrs. Heimarck was out of sight, however, my mother demanded that Jean finish her popsicle because one mightn't waste anything the minister's wife had bought. Mother watched, scowling. Then Mother actually spanked Jean and sent her to her room for the rest of the day. Mother was mortified that Jean had behaved so disgracefully, showing her emotions in front of the pastor's wife. Worry about how *she herself appeared* to the pastor's wife was more important to Mother than was the sadness and disappointment of her own daughter. The real irony is that if Mrs. Heimarck had known the true story—what opinion would she then have had of our "real" mother? I didn't get all of this at age 10, but I get it now and I will never lose it.

Sometimes a beautiful thing happens as we unlearn an old lie. Old truths in our lives get vivid to us—notably clearer: they become truths we now want to hang onto and honor. In my case, once I realized what a lie it was to believe that discussion is bad, boy did I begin to delight in the sheer pleasure that comes in the exchange of ideas. I learned to love the study of philosophy which questions just about everything. What a joy!

We can learn from our own pasts, from the memories of others, and from the stories of great literature. We can recognize in ourselves and in others qualities that we admire and qualities that we despise—and we can choose to become deeper. We can see how others choose in spots that we've been in and in spots that we haven't yet been in.

Here's how morality gets into what otherwise looks like merely cognitive process: this empathic inquiry can wake up the feel of things we really want to stand up for. The idea here is that we can develop *our own unified philosophy of life*. Every human being has the capacity for developing a unified philosophy. But here is a source of confusion: when we think about all the roles we play, citizen, worker, parent, child, spouse, church goer, coach, consumer—we may get the idea that we are a different person in each role. The truth is that with a unified philosophy of life we are the same person carrying out different jobs at different times.

Our "home self," our "work self," our "spiritual self," our "voting self," and our "humorous self" are all consistent parts of the same self. Developing a unified philosophy sounds so simple, but really very few members of *homo sapiens* actually do it.

One of the passionate pursuits of Social Work is to invite and instruct people of the world to discover their own latent philosophies.

—Cynthia Loveland

 Carol Bly is an author of books of short stories and essays, teacher of creative writing and public speaker—most recently at Hamm Psychiatric Clinic's Annual Conference, May 2003, and Dakota Wesleyan University, September 2003.

Carol Bly is writing consultant to the Minnesota School Social Workers' Association's Pamphlet Committee. Their most recent publication is Pamphlet #2, *A New Psychology for the Privileged Perpetrator.*

Bly's three most recent books are *Changing the Bully Who Rules the World,* 1996, *My Lord Bag of Rice,* 2000, both published by Milkweed Editions; and *Beyond the Writers Workshop: New Ways to Write Creative Nonfiction,* Random House (Anchor Books, 2001).

Three chapters of her in-progress novel, *Shelter Half,* have been published by *The Idaho Review* and *Prairie Schooner.*

Cynthia Loveland, MSW, ACSW, has worked as a Social Worker all of her adult life. After earning her MSW at the University of Minnesota she worked for nine years in county social service in rural Minnesota. Then the past 29 years have been spent working as a School Social Worker for the St. Paul Public Schools.

She has been active in professional and community organizations—including most recently serving as Secretary of the Board of the Minnesota Chapter of the National Association of Social Workers (NASW) and as Chair of the Pamphlet Committee of the Minnesota School Social Workers' Association (MSSWA).